Academic and Entrepreneurial Research

Academic and Entrepreneurial Research

The Consequences of Diversity in Federal Evaluation Studies

Ilene Nagel Bernstein
and
Howard E. Freeman

RUSSELL SAGE FOUNDATION   New York

PUBLICATIONS OF RUSSELL SAGE FOUNDATION

Russell Sage Foundation was established in 1907 by Mrs. Russell Sage for the improvement of social and living conditions in the United States. In carrying out its purpose the Foundation conducts research under the direction of members of the staff or in close collaboration with other institutions, and supports programs designed to develop and demonstrate productive working relations between social scientists and other professional groups. As an integral part of its operation, the Foundation from time to time publishes books or pamphlets resulting from these activities. Publication under the imprint of the Foundation does not necessarily imply agreement by the Foundation, its Trustees, or its staff with the interpretations or conclusions of the authors.

Russell Sage Foundation
230 Park Avenue, New York, N.Y. 10017

To Orville G. Brim, Jr.

Contents

Preface

Several years ago, when Francis Caro was commissioned by Russell Sage Foundation to edit a book of readings on evaluation research (Caro 1971), reviewers of his draft chapter outline suggested the book begin with some early articles in the field in order to give the reader a historical perspective. Dr. Caro complied and began the work with an article by A. Stephen Stephan (1935) which called for the experimental evaluation of Franklin D. Roosevelt's New Deal social programs. This little-known article is quite remarkable. Deletion of the term "New Deal" and substitution of the "Great Society" slogan would have made it timely in the 1960s and, while neither Presidents Nixon nor Ford developed a catchy phrase to describe their human-resources and social-welfare programs, the article is equally applicable today. The message is clear: unless policy-makers, social planners, and the public know the consequences of efforts at planned social change and social innovation, new, broad-scale programs of social action cannot be judged rationally.

Even in the 1930s, there were precedents for advocating the application of rigorous social methods to the assessment of social-action programs. Psychologists were beginning to undertake studies of an experimental character in and out of the laboratory. Stuart Dodd's (1934) classic water-boiling experiment in the Middle East was part of the sociological literature, and social planning was beginning to emerge as a professional activity rooted in the social sciences.

Certainly a case can be made for the historical continuity between the current level of evaluation-research activity and the development of social sciences over the past forty years or so in the United States. Contemporary psychology and sociology students still have at least some acquaintance with Newcomb's (1943) study of attitude change among girls at Bennington College, of Lippitt and White's study in the 1930s of the impact of authoritarian and democratic leadership styles on children's group relationships (Lippitt 1940), and of the research reports, too numerous to reference, of Kurt Lewin and his associates on social influence undertaken during the 1930s and 1940s. Then, too, there is the monumental applied-research program carried out by Stouffer and associates on American soldiers during World War II and the famous Western Electric Studies of the 1930s that contributed the term "Hawthorne effect" to the social science vocabulary (see Madge 1962 for a discussion of these two major research efforts).

The historical trajectory can be extended and updated. Delinquency-prevention programs, penal-rehabilitation efforts, psychotherapeutic and psychopharmacological treatments, public housing projects, and community organization activities are only some of the social action and intervention efforts that were scrutinized and evaluated by social scientists in the 1950s and 1960s.

Similarities also can be found in Stephan's 1930 statement and Campbell's 1969 call, as he put it, for an experimental approach to social reform. So, too, can the development of an increasingly sophisticated methodology be traced from early descriptions of field experiments to the still often-cited 1967 volume on principles and practice of evaluation research by Suchman, and now to the spate of books on evaluation research and program assessments that have appeared in the 1970s (for example, Freeman and Sherwood 1970; Schulberg et al. 1970; Weiss 1972; and Rossi and Williams 1972).

But enough of history! Indeed, the link between the concern over the past forty years of social science with social experiments, and the current assessment of social programs and extensive evaluation-research activities can easily be exaggerated, or at least obscure the qualitative difference: evaluation research is now a political tool. In this sense, it is a new social invention, one that, as Robert Merton has stated about all inventions, is "discovered" because of the social-structural circumstances of the times. Certainly it is not a zero-sum game in which political decisions concerning procedures, interventions, and treatments are implemented, or competing social programs are supported on the basis of evaluation research. Clearly these decisions do not depend solely on evaluation research studies. In fact, as Wholey et al. (1970) point out, there are few, if any, concrete illustrations of well-developed and carefully conducted evaluation studies that have been completed in time to affect directly either legislation or the short-range decision-making process of policy-makers. But, interestingly, it is the politician, the government official, and the social planner who now are the strongest advocates of evaluation research; it is not a social science lobby but those in responsible places who are the current sponsors of evaluation activities.

Currently it is mostly *doing* evaluation research studies, not their results, that provides the added impact to the complex political mosaic that surrounds important policy decisions. But even doing evaluation studies tailors thinking, shapes the style of program development, increases the influence of some persons and institutions, and decreases the power of others. Perhaps a few concrete illustrations will help: it was possible to justify heavy federal participation in "Sesame Street" partly because it was being evaluated, not because there were unequivocal findings of its social worth; advocates of a guaranteed annual wage were able to avoid the matter of it possibly being a disincentive to work because this matter was under experimental study; millions of dollars for experimental school programs were appropriated partly because it is reasonable to do so since these programs would be subject to evaluation.

The transition of evaluation research from a benign social science activity to a politically supported and politically motivated endeavor would be an interesting topic for a thorough social and political analysis. In part the transition stems from the desire of academicians to make evaluation research a political tool, and their ascendancy to consultative and less often, but increasingly, full-time participation in policy and planning roles. In part, it is because of the professionalization, with considerable conceptual and technical background in the social sciences, of both career and politically appointed public servants. In part, it is because of the growing number of congressmen and other elected officials with social science training as undergraduates and in law schools who have become charmed with what to them is a new idea. And, in part, it is because of the sheer size, political sensitiveness, and competition for scarce monies to support human-resource programs and social-welfare services. All of these have helped to transform evaluation research into a political tool.

There is no need to belabor the defects in the human condition and the social environment of the country. The question is—what can be done? The answer: innovate, experiment, and evaluate, for these very processes bring with them a certain amount of needed comfort, sanguineness, and time. Perhaps, too, they may serve as a detour from head-on confrontation with radical modes of social change. This is of course a one-sided view; the other side is that the *promise* of evaluation research as a policy-making input is a necessary evolutionary stage in the development of rational policy-making, and that the *products* of such investigations will subsequently be the important input.

There are in fact some glimmerings that, as a nation, we are moving in the direction of using the results of well-conducted, publicly scrutinized evaluation studies in the development of social programs, whether they be psychotherapy in prisons as a means of reducing recidivism (Kassebaum, Ward, and Wilner 1972), or of public housing as a solution to the alienation and social problems of the poor (Wilner et al. 1962). Sometimes the results open up, or at least serve to help continue, the debate on important social issues, such as the value of television as a compensatory educational activity (Cook et al. 1975). In isolated and admittedly often less sweeping ways, studies have pointed out the positive value of efforts, such as the worth of drugs in the community adjustment of mental patients or of programmed-learning instruction in educating retarded children. But, in any balanced assessment, given the considerable costs, the products of evaluation research have *not* made that much of a difference in the "total picture." One very possible consequence of a continued failure of the results of evaluation research to have a demonstrable impact on policy and program development is disenchantment by its now strong advocates.

The present study, frankly, was pragmatically motivated. It was originated, implemented, supported, and published by a foundation devoted to the utilization of social science and to the proposition that social science can contribute to social-policy development, social-action efforts, and social change. Because of its commitment, Russell Sage Foundation's antennae are continuously turned to the developing and shifting links between the social science academy and the policymaker and planner, particularly at the federal level. The awakened political interest in evaluation research was easily perceived. More than that, a number of Foundation staff members had nurtured it in their advisory and consultative activities with national commissions, and with panels and groups in several departments of the federal executive branch. It was apparent by 1970 that evaluation research had become an unstudied industry with a vast consortium of large and small profit-making corporations, nonprofit-making groups, university research centers, and independent entrepreneurs—both in and out of the academic environment—engaged in assessing social-action programs.

At considerable cost, many of the national, regional, state, and local social-development programs are now being scrutinized and "evaluated" in one way or another. It is equally clear that, from the standpoint of the results provided by investigators and what we knew of the utilization of evaluation research, the returns from supporting evaluation-research endeavors have been slim. Federal officials—both those sophisticated in social science lore and those without such background, evaluation researchers themselves, and persons more detached because of their academic or otherwise insulated positions—are dismayed that the industry continues to operate mostly at the promise rather than product level. Accordingly, Russell Sage Foundation, as described in its recent Annual Reports, launched a program to improve the state of evaluation research. It included the development of improved methodologies, the support of special training in evaluation research, and "evaluations of evaluations" in order to make visible the strengths and weaknesses of current important studies.

One of our earliest discoveries was that no one really knew in any systematic and detailed way about the volume of evaluation-research activity, the sources of support, the characteristics of the organizations, the persons doing the work, and the analytical methods employed. There were varying and often divergent views on the virtues and deficits of different funding arrangements, types of research organizations, and the resultant quality of work and its policy impact. Thus, we undertook this study to review and evaluate one year's experience of direct support for evaluation. Our aim was simple: to describe and criticize the evaluation-research industry, at least as it relates to federal programs. The intent was not to muckrake but to direct attention to the current status of work, and to stimulate the development and utilization of evaluation research.

The objectives and procedures of our study are provided in some detail in the first few chapters. One additional point, however, should be made here. As we began to think about the design of the study, it became evident that there was little precedent on which to fall back. There simply is not much of a sociology of the social sciences, especially of applied social science, that could guide our study. Neither sufficient conceptualization nor methods exist on how to appraise social-research undertakings. Thus, the temptation has been great to convert the investigation into much more of an academic project than was originally intended. While we have tried to stick to the original intent of providing a description and critique of a relatively unexplored field of activity— an industry if you will—we cannot help but feel that this study contributes too to the slender knowledge that the social scientists have about themselves and their work. At least, we hope it may stimulate more inquiries about ourselves.

In order to carry out the study, cooperation was essential from a large number of groups and persons in government and in evaluation-research organizations. Virtually all, ranging from persons in the highest levels of various federal departments to computer programmers in different agencies, gave freely of their time and experience. Names are too numerous to mention, though that does not in any way diminish our sincere appreciation. Likewise colleagues in and outside of the Foundation were generous with technical advice and helpful in "opening doors." Again, any list would be unduly long and possibly incomplete, and so a general acknowledgment of gratitude must therefore suffice.

Before concluding, I should explain how the work was done. The study was conceived by Orville G. Brim, Jr., then president of Russell Sage Foundation (now president of the Foundation for Child Development), and myself. We did much of the early spadework and the preliminary design. Ilene Bernstein joined us as the questionnaire was being developed, and from that point on was responsible on a day-to-day basis for the implementation of the study, as well as for most of the data analysis.

At the time the study was initiated, Patricia Rieker, now of the University of North Carolina, was interested in problems of utilization and dissemination of evaluaton research. She designed a number of items for this purpose that are included in our questionnaire, and undertook face-to-face interviews with a small subgroup of the investigators. Her work will be the subject of a separate report, but her contribution to the overall study is acknowledged here. Ilene Bernstein and I, however, are solely responsible for the contents of this volume.

HOWARD E. FREEMAN

January 1975

CHAPTER ONE

The Evaluation-Research Endeavor

There is no commonly accepted definition of the term "evaluation research." As we use the term here, it is the systematic study of the operation of social-action, treatment, or intervention programs, and of their impact. Ideally, the goals of evaluation research are twofold: first, to supply information that allows policy-makers, planners, and professionals to make rational decisions about social-development and human-resource programs and thus to maximize the expenditure of economic and human resources; and, second, to add to knowledge available about social and interpersonal behavior and the social environment, and to explicate and refine the practice principles that underlie programming efforts.

In a broad context, evaluation research can be seen as a major social-change force. It is part of a general perspective on how to order communal activities relative to improving the human condition. Campbell, in a recent interview, succinctly sums up a viewpoint he has promoted for almost two decades and which has attracted many advocates:

> The experimenting society I have in mind would initiate programs and realistically evaluate the outcomes, in the case of failure going on to new problems and in the case of success retaining these as policy, using the best of science to design programs (in Salasin 1973, p. 12).

Both as a narrow decision-making and management tool and as part of a broader social-planning and policy perspective, evaluation-research efforts are now an integral part of most programs in the numerous federal

1

agencies that share responsibility for welfare and human-resource programs. But the federal establishment is not a monolithic organization and the character and implementation of evaluation efforts varies greatly from one federal group to another. At the outset, then, it is important to place evaluation research in the context of the contemporary federal scene, for our concern is with the state of affairs regarding evaluation-research efforts supported directly by the federal agencies and departments.

THE HUMAN-RESOURCE SECTOR OF THE FEDERAL GOVERNMENT

Neither the most competent group of economic analysts nor the most creative team of organizational scientists could unravel fully the structure and activities of the federal government in the broad area of what can be termed "human-resource and social-welfare programs." Every one of the federal departments is committed to a multitude of programs of social services, education, health, public security, and the like. There are also a number of independent agencies with specific charges, such as the moribund Office of Economic Opportunity (OEO) and the expanding Environmental Protection Agency (EPA). Moreover, between and within many executive departments, there are often programs that overlap in their objectives, their intervention efforts, and the target populations they serve.

Equally important is the fact that there are wide variations in the administration of programs: some are undertaken directly from Washington, some by regional federal offices, and still others by states and localities with monies in whole or in part provided by Washington. Accountability differs too. Some programs require detailed reports on persons and groups served, evidence of results, and details of fiscal expenditures; others only demand an affidavit that funds were spent as they were supposed to be expended. Additionally, within and between agencies, there is variation in the span and scope of expenditure authority. Some groups, although part of executive departments, are virtually autonomous because of the legislation that surrounds their activities, and the administrative and political traditions that exist; others are closely linked and directed by the office of the secretary of the particular executive department. In many cases "middle management" virtually has complete authority and the upper echelons operate solely as a formal certifying body. For example, the National Institutes of Health are part of the Department of Health, Education and Welfare. But even in terms of budget, and certainly in day-to-day operations, they are virtually independent of the Secretary's office. Indicative of this is that the National Institutes have, for a long time, had direct lobbying ties to Congress and independent program-development links to the White House.

Briefly then, there is no single national human-resource and social-welfare program, but rather a number of relatively independent and often competing activities between and within departments. This state of affairs is not altogether negative; it is believed by some that a moderate level of competition is healthy in the federal establishment just as it is in the production and vending of, for example, automobiles. But it does have implications, to be discussed subsequently, for the development, funding, and implementation of evaluation research.

Another frequent observation has to do with current perceptions of the efficacy and utility of various program efforts. Few major programs are above criticism; few are regarded as perfectly developed and useful. For example, even the generally highly regarded insurance-principled Social Security Program has been criticized because of the amount of payments, the different options men and women have with respect to age of retirement, and the failure to treat incipient disability problems preventively. Most programs, in fact, are strongly criticized by Congress, the general public, and especially the persons who run them, and are believed to be in need of drastic revision. The network of income security and housing programs for the poor are only two glaring examples.

There are few people, regardless of party affiliation or political ideology, who enthusiastically support the existing federal programs. Billions of dollars are spent each year by the federal establishment for programs that are often questionably administered, controlled, and coordinated. The programs are frequently judged and harshly assessed by a variety of persons and agencies according to wide-ranging criteria. This then is the backdrop of current interest and the high level of activity in which evaluation research takes place.

WHY DO EVALUATION RESEARCH?

In the preface of this volume evaluation research is described as a political device, particularly at the federal level. Advocacy of evaluation research by politicians and policy-makers is based on a number of related concerns with the costs and effectiveness of the panorama of social-development and human-resource programs. For many, evaluation research is a management tool, an input into the mosaic that surrounds decision-making on support of social programs. It is clear that giving the most expensive services to persons or, correspondingly, spending an almost infinite number of dollars is not useful or wise in the face of limited resources and a virtually unlimited array of social concerns. For example, we know that long-term, $40-per-hour psychotherapy is not the solution to the mental-health problems of the country. Moreover, the expensive public programs, conceived to restore persons to the work force, have not reduced the staggering size of the welfare population. Thus, for some, evaluation research is regarded as a type of extended cost-benefit analysis with management implications. It is, for example, deemed appropriate to examine the expenditure of funds used for training workers by the Department of Labor in terms of "results," in addition to measuring dollar expenditures and cost per trainee in order to obtain measures of program utility. What is important is the addition of the idea of the cost per trainee completing a program and employed in the craft for which he is trained. In the simplest terms, evaluation research is a means by which an agency can examine what it is getting in return for the resources expended.

Moreover, it is clear that programs operate in competition with each other, particularly for economic resources. Evaluation research can thus be an input into making decisions about support of competing programs. For example, in the health field, some experts stress the use of home care for the chronically ill and aged population; others favor the expansion of nursing-home care. Evaluation research potentially can assist in deciding which program receives the major push. Also, several agencies with somewhat different philosophies may have programs in the same field. For example, programs of training of school social workers may be supported by both the Office of Education and the National Institute of Mental Health. Decisions on assignment or responsibility to a particular agency for activities can be based in part on measures of effective program implementation and outcome.

Finally, it may be important to assess the side effects of alternative programs sharing common goals. For example, the substitution of a guaranteed annual wage for public welfare payments raises questions about whether or not the former will be a disincentive to work. In fact, this is not a hypothetical illustration but a major focus of the costly University of Wisconsin–Mathematica guaranteed-income experiment. Research efforts may be useful when comparing and contrasting innovative new programs which have been proposed to replace traditional ones.

Although the political basis of evaluation research has been stressed, many evaluation studies also are initiated by nongovernmental sources. Evaluation research studies are a means of assessing practice programs such as a new intervention approach to delinquency control, an innovative teacher-training program for urban educators, and so on. Many of these evaluations are begun by practicing professionals and their organizations, and may be supported by either governmental groups or private foundations.

Indeed, the federal government has encouraged such efforts, usually termed "research-demonstration programs," and a variety of agencies have funding authority to support them. Such programs usually are either local or statewide in character, and are supported both to uncover innovative ideas with broad generalization potential and to encourage inputs from non-Washington groups. Generally, federal agencies stimulate work in different areas at different times by "inviting" proposals in fields such as mental retardation, aging, or drug control.

It should be noted that many so-called research-demonstration projects are hardly evaluations. Rather, the funds are provided for operating programs that are sometimes innovative and sometimes dressed up to appear new. Support is obtained on the pretext that special funding is warranted since the programs are "experimental." The evaluation components of many of these projects are most superficial.

Finally, social scientists with primarily academic interests submit evaluation studies. They usually do so either to study practice and program ideas that they have dressed up with a social science framework or to clarify hypotheses in their areas of academic interest through the use of field experiments. Agencies such as the National Institute of Mental Health and the National Science Foundation encourage such submissions and often support them. Again, it should be noted that the motives may not be entirely pure. Some social scientists are dedicated to policy-oriented research and to experimental studies related to innovation and change. But social scientists also respond to the need to support their research, their students, and themselves, and are alert to areas where federal interest and funding opportunities exist.

THE CURRENT STATE OF EVALUATION RESEARCH

Despite the potential use of evaluation, the actual impact remains meager at best. The possibilities of evaluation research are appreciated. But, as already noted, there have been few cases of actual effective utilization of evaluation research for expected purposes. Wholey et al. (1970) list a number of reasons for this state of affairs. The reasons can be classified into three groups.

First, there are issues of a methodological and organizational sort. There is not only a lack of sufficient methodological know-how and, sometimes. too little competence on the part of research investigators, but there are difficulties in securing the necessary cooperation from groups or programs to be evaluated. Moreover, the time-frame of political decisions, in comparison with the period necessary to complete and report studies, results in the completion of many evaluations after decisions have in fact been made.

Second, at all levels within the federal establishment, there are problems in developing specifications for and monitoring evaluation research. Due to the way most agencies and executive departments are structured, the decision-makers themselves have little money for evaluation studies. For example, at the time this study was undertaken, in the Department of Health, Education and Welfare (HEW) there was a deputy assistant secretary for planning and evaluation who literally had no funds for research activities. His role, although he was the arm of the Secretary, was to try to plan, coordinate, and then influence groups within HEW to undertake competent evaluations. In many cases, the Secretary's Office had little to do with deciding what studies were done, and practically no control over how they were undertaken. When implemented, they were most often undertaken by the organizations who were operating and responsible for the programs. This situation has changed somewhat and in 1974 about $45 million for research was available in the Secretary's Office. About $15 million was earmarked for evaluation research, although only $8 million was spent. The change came from assuming responsibilities formerly in OEO, and by "taxing" subordinate program groups.

In addition, with a few notable exceptions, the various groups in the federal departments do not have staffs with the experience or competence to develop the specifications for evaluation-research studies, to select investigators and research organizations, and to monitor their implementation and completion. The legislative branch and their arm for accountability —the General Accounting Office (GAO)—as well as the executive branch with its Office of Management and Budget do not regularly have large amounts of funds or the professional manpower for evaluation-research activities, at least at the level where they can initiate their own original field studies (Staats 1974). Except in the case of special appropriations and projects of the fairly independent groups—e.g., the National Institutes of Health and the Office of Economic Opportunity—evaluation-research activities are intertwined with operating responsibilities and not directly linked to the political influentials and the professionals who function on a policy- and decision-making level. Moreover, there are major problems in the communication of the results of studies. The persons doing the work and the consumers simply do not operate on the same wavelength in terms of language, priorities to be emphasized, and the like. Neither the evaluation researchers themselves nor the federal staff generally are equipped to turn research into action which affects policy.

Third, there is neither a federal evaluation policy nor a set of requirements and guidelines regarding what constitutes an appropriate evaluation. This lack has severe consequences. It results in a failure to enforce any standardized set of evaluation requirements, even when present in legislation. In a number of cases, for example, the Office of Management and

Budget (OMB) has an obligation, prior to the release of additional funds, to ascertain if the past period of activities has been "evaluated." If the program is liked by OMB and the White House, almost anything can pass as meeting this requirement, for there is no explicit definition of what constitutes an evaluation. Conversely, if a program is disliked, it can be given a "hard time" because of a label of an "inadequate" evaluation. When there are no clearly agreed upon standards, subjective opinions based on other vested interests may easily reign.

More importantly, perhaps, in the absence of a federal evaluation policy evaluations rarely take place early enough. An intelligence unit is needed that proposes and organizes evaluations of programs prior to their formal legislative or executive consideration or efforts to terminate them by Congress, the White House, or one of the departments. The guaranteed annual wage proposition, for example, should have been evaluated as an alternative to public welfare in the very early 1960s, not a decade later; "Sesame Street" should have been evaluated before it became a national program, not after it was on the air nationwide. An evaluation-planning unit needs to promote evaluation before decision-making is imminent, even if many program studies for evaluation purposes never receive further attention.

INSTIGATION AND SUPPORT OF EVALUATION STUDIES

There is, in general, a mixed impetus for the initiation and funding of social science research activities. A number of agencies exist with authority to provide funds for social research, such as the National Science Foundation, the National Institutes of Health, and the National Institute of Education. Most of the available funds are not for across-the-board support of research activities, but are restricted to a set of areas which have been deemed to require investigation because of national interests, and because academicians, scientists, and policy-makers have advised agencies that there are gaps in knowledge that hinder the prospect for improving the welfare of the country.

There is continuous criticism about the restrictions placed on available funds. Many support the view that the specification of an important research problem, well-grounded in theory and with a well-developed methodology, should be the sole basis for federal support of social research. The counterargument is, of course, that there is an obligation to spend public funds in ways consistent with the needs and aspirations of the general population of the country.

It is recognized by funding agencies that what might be referred to as "applied research" rests heavily on the continual development and improvement in basic knowledge and the refinement of methodological techniques. The funds provided for these purposes, however, are relatively modest in comparison with amounts available to persons who tailor their research so that it includes matters of policy concerns and who can make a "case" of its practical utility. For example, a psychologist may be interested in the development of knowledge on operant conditioning; by designing a study so that the subjects of the experiment are mentally retarded children, the investigator increases the number of potential funding sources, since several agencies within the federal establishment can justify support of the research because of the "spin-off" and potential utility of the work. In practice, much of social science research is supported by arrangements that allow the interests of social scientists and funding parties to converge, or by "trade-offs" in which investigators include or expand their research to take into account the interest of funding agencies.

The Grant Process

Since many agencies in different departments are involved and have authority to support social research, including evaluation studies, a single description of the process of the development of problems and their fundings is impossible. A major and important distinction must, however, be made between grants and contracts. The grant process of the National Institute of Mental Health (NIMH) is illustrative of the formal procedures used in the award of research funds. Many persons in the social sciences and in government believe that the procedures in NIMH and the several National Institutes of Health are an extremely effective way of operating. Other agencies have less structured and consistent ways of awarding grants. The NIMH has a general mandate that includes the support of investigations on a variety of problems in mental health, broadly defined to include a wide range of social and community problems. To a certain extent, the areas believed to be priorities of the legislative branch tailor the general research program of the institute, although in actuality many of the expressed interests of the Congressmen have been stimulated by formal and informal contacts and by influence and pressure from persons within the NIMH, members of the psychiatry profession, and social scientists. In short, the Congressmen have been told what is important.

In any event, the priorities are expressed not only in terms of the policy statements of the agency but are reflected in the way the administration and operation of the research program is structured. The structure includes three important elements: First, the NIMH includes a number of units with specific charges, so that there are specific groups to administer and stimulate programs on the effective utilization of community mental-health centers, the use of paraprofessional workers, and so on. These groups not only have individual budget allocations for their operations, but the personnel selected for key positions in them operate to further shape the program. Second, there is a national advisory council made up of policy-makers, influential citizens, university administrators, and senior researchers who undertake final reviews of research projects and recommend their support or their rejection to the director of NIMH (and in theory to his superiors although they rarely are directly involved). Third, there are decision-making groups referred to as "study sections." Each is composed of about twelve social and medical scientists, usually with strong records as researchers and research administrators. Efforts are made to balance study sections in terms of discipline, professional orientation, and region of location, as well as age, ethnic background, and sex.

Study sections generally meet three or four times a year, review applications submitted by social investigators, and decide which ones should be recommended to the advisory council. In addition to the recommendation, study sections provide a detailed evaluation explaining the significance of the problem, the design of the study, and its relationship to various problem areas. Based on their overall judgment, a priority is assigned to each proposal. In many cases, prior to the final review, selected members of the study section or outside consultants visit the site of the investigation to meet with the investigator and his or her staff. While the role of such "site visitors" is theoretically evaluative, often they take on a consultative function as well. The site visitors usually have expertise and knowledge in the proposed area of work, and they often serve as valuable advisers.

Naturally, the persons who make up a study section influence the projects which will be approved and the priority scores that each will be given. Thus, the selection of study-section members shapes the NIMH program. In addition, each study section has an executive secretary whose formal role is to implement its work and to be its administrative coordinator. The executive secretary has both obvious and subtle ways of influencing the decision as to which projects will be supported. For example, in many study sections, it is the executive secretary who decides which members visit a particular project for a face-to-face discussion with the investigator. The executive secretary also has at his or her disposal information about past grants that have been approved and disapproved in the area and by the agency. By volunteering or withholding such information, the deliberations of the study section may be affected.

Then too, study sections, including the executive secretaries, often meet to discuss among themselves priorities and research emphases, in terms of the mandate they have been given to review grants in a particular area. At times, there are senior members of the NIMH staff included in these discussions as well. These meetings are another means by which NIMH informally influences the direction of its program.

It is important to note here that usually the executive secretaries of study sections, and many of the senior staff members of NIMH, are themselves well-trained social scientists or persons with research experience in psychiatry and the social sciences. Many have worked in universities and research centers, and have made their own contributions to research literature. Executive secretaries may be extremely active in stimulating the academic research community to think about undertaking investigations in areas deemed to be of high priority to the institute. In addition, senior institute staff members also have their own networks of contact with investigators and use them to create demands for funds in a particular area. On occasion, formal announcements are made of special areas of concern in which there is not enough activity to suit the institute. The academic community is quite sensitive to the current and emerging interests to institutes like NIMH, and there is an informal communication network and considerable cooperation among academic persons whose long-term relationships to the funding agency make them part of its "extended family."

In general, the "study-section system" works remarkably well. The professionalized and academic character of the internal staff of the institute and the peer-review system operate with reasonable fairness, high standards, and relative immunity from political influence. From time to time, the process is criticized on the grounds that study-group members and staff are a coalition that limit opportunities for either unknown investigators or highly unusual research ideas. Also, some argue that the entire process and the research supported is too "academic." On balance, however, the process is functional and respected for successfully doing what it was created to do.

Many agencies in the federal establishment have the authority to award grants. The grant procedure in the National Institutes of Health, the National Institute of Mental Health, and similar groups is the most formalized one, and regarded by the academic research community as the best. Some agencies use variants of this procedure. The National Science Foundation (NSF) makes use of consultants who provide written evaluations of grants, which then are collated by a staff person who fulfills a role similar to that of an executive secretary in the NIMH. Sometimes the consultants also meet together as well. These reviews and group assessments are then judged by key internal people at NSF. Other federal agencies, rather than maintaining permanent study sections with members who serve for set terms, make use of ad hoc committees for the same purpose.

In other agencies, such as the Office of Education, which have grant authority, there is much less of a competitive process. Most of the approved projects are encouraged by internal staff members, and proposals are reviewed in a less formal and consistent manner. Other groups such as the defunct Office of Economic Opportunity, the Social Rehabilitation Service of HEW, and the Department of Justice make some use of outside advisors as well as internal staff in making grant decisions. But the process probably is less universal and competitive than the "model process" described.

Once grants are made, usually to persons located in universities or other nonprofit research centers, investigators are left very much on their own with the exception of fiscal auditing. They are encouraged to provide information on their work and to disseminate the results of their study via professional journals and book-length monographs. The Institutes, such as that of Mental Health, also devote considerable energy to making the results of studies available via house-sponsored publications so as to increase the dissemination of the results. Final reports are usually required but often are regarded largely as a formality.

There are few controls on the investigators and what they do with grant funds after an award is made. Perhaps the strongest controls are executed by the peer-group review committee; study-section members are usually well known in their disciplines and areas of work and their assessments are important to investigators. Investigators know that peer-group review committees use past performance as a major criterion in judging future performance, i.e., new applications. Indeed, every investigator has a dossier of the deliberations of study sections on the past applications that he or she has submitted. Clearly an individual who has a strong record of approvals and high priorities for past applications is favored when his or her new application is examined. Moreover, the investigator who can submit an extensive bibliography and copies of high-quality publications from past grants is in an enviable position.

In terms of evaluation research, some evaluations are supported by grants submitted at the initiative of individual investigators and/or their organizations. However, the grant process also is used to support work that either an agency, such as NIMH, deems important or that is of interest to professional associations, groups of practitioners, or policy-makers within the federal government. In such circumstances, the regular review process usually occurs but there may be considerable presubmission "collaboration" between the funding institute and a particular investigator in the development of the grant application. Sometimes, formally or informally, the study section is informed of the interest of the institute or other groups in a particular application. While such efforts to influence decision-making are sometimes regarded negatively by study-section members, in general they comply and approve the grant as long as it is reasonably developed both theoretically and methodologically.

In summary, grants are characterized by having been initiated by the investigator. They are awarded after peer review and often on a competitive basis where proposals on related problems are judged against each other. Also, there are, in general, few restrictions outside of budgetary ones on the activities of investigators working with grants. The emphasis is on producing papers for academic journals or books and monographs for a broad community of persons rather than for internal use. Moreover, unlike contracts, the grant programs of the federal agencies, or at least of the Institutes, tend to be monitored and coordinated by persons with considerable disciplinary training overall.

Contracts

In addition to grant authority, many agencies may fund research by contracts. Some agencies have both authorities, others have only one or the other. When agencies have only grant authority they may tend to use some of the money as if it were contract funds; likewise, when agencies have only contract authority, they use some of the funds for a quasi-grant program. But in principle the difference is an important one; contracts are provided when an agency, either on its own or because of executive or legislative instructions and influence, deems it important to undertake a piece of research. Under the contract system, the general rule is that the agency—for example, the Manpower Administration of the Department of Labor—draws up a set of project specifications which state in varying detail the research they wish to accomplish and thus will support.

Most contract award actions, in theory at least, are required to be competitive. Contracts are advertised and individuals are invited to bid for them or at least secure more information and specifications about proposed research contracts. The information released often includes details on the form the research proposal and budget should take and the submission date.

The review process varies greatly from agency to agency. Some use a review system similar to the study-section idea described in the discussion of grants. Others use an internal group structure, with the in-house group making all decisions. Cost, of course, is one factor taken into account, but the decision-making group also considers the past performance of the bidder, his or her research capabilities, and sometimes the methodological rigor and competence of the proposal submitted. In general, there is much more variation in the composition of the groups that make decisions on award of contracts than of grants. In many cases, decision-making is dominated by administrators within agencies, who have neither the research background nor experience to judge proposals from a technical standpoint. Sometimes outside consultants and review groups are used for this reason.

But there still is an essential difference. Since the agency has a strong interest and sometimes a legal responsibility to undertake the work advertised, it is not usually a question of judging a proposal in competition with other proposals that may be in the same area but which are substantially different in specific problem foci. Rather, the process is one of judging which of the *available* applicants should receive the award for a specific piece of work. In some of the areas, work is stimulated by the social science and professional communities, in the same sense that they influence the priorities and policy concerns of institutes like NIMH. For the most part, however, it is either a political decision or a response to a directive from the executive branch or Congress that shapes the areas to be investigated under contract research. Further, most often a relatively short period—often less than three months—is allotted for the preparation of research proposals, and generally the time in which the work must be accomplished is tightly set. Additionally, contracts often include provisions for detailed interim reporting dates. Contract work occasionally is subjected to considerable surveillance and direction by the supporting agency as the research goes on.

In practice, overlapping but nevertheless different groups of organizations maintain interest in contract and grant research. This is, in part, because of the difference in the intent of the twin mechanisms and in the nature of the funding and decision-making processes. There are many profit-making organizations, large and small, who frequently respond to the initiatives set out by the various agencies. Some of these organizations are either organized or owned by academic researchers who moonlight in profit-making consortia. Other organizations employ academicians on a part-time or leave basis. Many of the larger ones have additional departments that engage in consultative work for government and private industry and operate human-service programs in particular areas. Occasionally, university research organizations and somewhat more often nonprofit groups respond to contract-research opportunities.

Although strictly speaking anyone can bid for a contract, most federal units have a preselected group of suppliers. To some extent, traditions maintain these relationships. A group that has worked congenially with an agency may subtly or formally be given "credit" for past work in the decision-making process that surrounds the award. This is particularly so when an internal decision-making group composed of federal employees decides on awards. At other times, the number of contractors is restricted because only a few have the special expertise required to do work in a particular area and they consistently submit the proposals that are approved, each time enhancing their reputation for competence within a federal agency. Finally, sometimes certain specifications are written into the contract which conform to the competence and interests of one or a few potential bidders.

This is often a matter of realism and expediency, and there is no reason to necessarily be negative about this procedure. In some ways, it is similar to the actions of peer-group review committees who look at the past records and performance of applicants for grants.

In addition to competitive contracts, on occasion contracts are given out on a sole-source basis; that is, a particular organization is selected and arrangements are made to fund a piece of work desired by an agency. This most often occurs when either time pressures or a scarcity of competing organizations is apparent. In many cases, agencies protect themselves from possible accusations of corruption or bias by having outside groups review the proposed work and sometimes by having them assist in the monitoring of sole-source contracts.

In summation, many evaluation-research projects are funded through contracts. While there is a great deal of overlap between the mechanisms of grants and contracts, it is important to take into account the basic differences described above, especially when trying to examine the scope of evaluation research with direct federal support. The initiation and implementation processes of evaluation research supported by grants and contracts, and how they differ, are thus key areas of concern in this study.

WHO DOES THE WORK?

Persons who engage in evaluation research range markedly in experience and training. For the most part, they have some academic credentials in either the social sciences or one of the related practicing professions. The major disciplinary areas include economics, sociology, and psychology, if the person is from a social science discipline; medicine, public health, law, and social work are the practicing professions most represented. Persons engaged at various levels in evaluation research may have doctorates, master's, or bachelor's degrees. Not only does their formal training differ in discipline and depth, but their past experience in related research also is quite varied. Persons without higher degrees may have decades of experience in the areas in which they work, or new Ph.D.'s with limited research experience may be the key persons on a project.

It is hard for the federal establishment to make judgments on criteria of research competence. This is not only because of the difficulty of equating experience and educational training, but because in the social sciences and the practicing professions there are wide variations in the scope and levels of research training provided in different fields and universities. Moreover, whether or not it is an academic organization, often there is considerable difference between the person whose name appears as the one responsible for a particular project and the person who actually does the work. For example, in some of the large academic research centers, the director of a particular unit may consistently be listed as the principal investigator of projects although the amount of supervision he or she gives is minimal. This is true in the profit-making groups as well. Further, there is considerable mobility in organizations in which the evaluation research takes place; the person who initially begins a project, particularly through a contract, may leave, be promoted, or reassigned to other work, and someone else may take over. While some agencies require permission for such personnel changes, others do not.

Not only are there wide variations in the background and experience of the persons who do the work, but the organizations with which they are affiliated also differ greatly in size, mission, and the extent to which they are concerned with doing the research or getting the award. This is true for all groups involved. Many graduate departments and university research centers rely heavily on grants and contracts to support their faculty, to provide funds and research experience for graduate students, and the like. Nonprofit, independent research groups are mainly dependent on "soft-money" federal support for their programs. In this sense, university centers and nonprofit organizations are not too different from the profit-making sector, except that the budget categories are somewhat dissimilar. Profit-making corporations clearly would be out of business if they did not fare well in the competition for research awards and so their motivation is probably higher than that of the established academic centers. Thus the former are less likely to be as selective in the awards they accept to obtain funds.

Another dimension is the relationship between the evaluation researcher and the program or activity that is being evaluated. At one extreme are the cases in which evaluation investigators and program personnel are completely independent. Indeed, at times, contracting officials and granting agencies make great efforts to be sure that there are no formal or informal relationships between the evaluation research group and the persons active in administering a particular program. At the other extreme, there are evaluation studies that are an integral part of action and service programs. For example, an organization may receive an evaluation-research grant in order to assess a program that is underway in its own agency. At times, funds for both the service part and the research part of the project are built into the same contract or grant. This is usually the case in "research-demonstration" programs. Somewhere between the two notions of an "independent evaluation" and an evaluation as a part of an action program, are contracts or grants that are provided for groups that have some degree of collaboration with the staff of the program or action agency. In some cases, there is joint planning of the evaluation and the action programs undertaken. In other cases, the evaluation group may actually "work for" the action group.

Also, as has been described, the role of the funding agency varies greatly. Persons within the funding agency may be active partners in either the evaluation program, the action program, or both; or their responsibilities may be limited to surveillance of ongoing activities. In still other cases they only make certain that the expenditures are appropriate and they "read" the end product of the work. Both the characteristics of the persons doing the work and the organizational arrangements are important dimensions that will be examined in trying to understand the evaluation activities of the federal government.

THE NATURE OF EVALUATION RESEARCH

There is considerable difference of opinion as to what constitutes evaluation research. From one standpoint, any information or assessment that allows one to reach decisions on programs, treatments, and/or interventions can be considered to be evaluation research. Much of what takes place under the guise of evaluation research only can be classified as such in terms of this broad definition.

There are agencies and programs in which evaluation research consists of what may be regarded as the application of conventional wisdom or "common sense." For example, if it is repeatedly observed that large numbers of children in some schools do not bring their lunch, and if a school lunch program then is initiated and the children eat the food, the latter fact becomes the "common-sense" evaluation.

It is important, of course, not to make too strong a case about the inappropriateness of "conventional-wisdom evaluations." First, in many instances they are right; second, given the resources, methodological difficulties, and time pressures, often this is all that can be done. The problem is, however, that many such efforts lead to faulty conclusions. For example, take the case just noted: if the parents of the children are indeed desperate for funds and consequently provide inadequate diets for their families, the knowledge that their children are receiving a meal in school can result in a redistribution of the food provided family members at home, such that a school lunch program can become not a supplement to a normal diet, but rather, just a substitute for what they would have received at home at different hours of the day.

A second type of activity often referred to as evaluation research is the judgment as to whether or not certain activities, treatments, and inter-

attempting to assess the effect of counseling programs in improving the mental health of young adults.

CHARACTERISTICS OF THE EVALUATION STUDY

As part of this study we sought information on the elements that characterize evaluation research, including the problem foci, the level of complexity of the study, and the theoretical framework of the investigation. The dimension simplest to describe is the substantive foci of the action programs that were evaluated. Some 15 percent were in the welfare area, 22 percent in health, 16 percent in mental health, 16 percent in education, 13 percent in income security and manpower, 15 percent in public safety, and 3 percent in housing. Interestingly, while there were more individual evaluations focused on health or mental-health programs than on other areas, there was more money directed toward evaluations of income security, housing, or welfare programs than to other problem concerns; one-half of all the awards with budgets of $150,000 or more were awarded to evaluate programs aimed at ameliorating these three problems. An example is an evaluation of the effectiveness of a settlement house in increasing income security of persons by providing educational and vocational classes. This particular research endeavor had a budget of nearly $504,000. Similarly, a one-year study assessing the impact of a particular community-referral process for welfare recipients to vocational programs cost $125,000. Perhaps this pattern reflects the intensive concern with "equality" and the areas of income security, housing, and welfare during the days of the "Great Society" program and the Kennedy-Johnson administrations. In the late 1960s, programs aimed at urban renewal, income maintenance, and social welfare flourished much as had the health and mental-health programs in the early 1960s.

Turning to the level of complexity, a point to note is that so many of the programs evaluated were focused on more than one problem area. Apparently planned intervention programs as attempts to direct social change are complex in that they often seek changes on several levels. Among studies in such fields as health, work training, and so on, many defined educational goals and income security as secondary interests. It appears that evaluation-research efforts often are tied to broadly rather than narrowly circumscribed action programs. As such, they are probably extremely difficult to carry out well, for when the research context is broadened, the number of external factors that must be considered increases.

Still another dimension related to the complexity of evaluation research is that many programs, in addition to having several foci, attempt to affect multiple groups, i.e., there are multiple targets for change. As such, the evaluation-research design often needs to study and sample more than one population. We asked each investigator whether the study included, as one of the units examined, "deviant persons," "persons administering services," and "organizational and territorial units."[3] Interestingly, 39 percent indicated that their studies examined two of these units, e.g., retarded children and physical therapists, or physical therapists and the organization of the hospital providing services.

Some 68 percent of all studies cited that one of the units studied, regardless of whether it was the only unit or not, was made up of deviant or problem persons. This, coupled with the fact that multiple foci and targets are involved, lends further support to the discussions in the literature that stress the complexity of evaluation research. First, having to sample two or more populations sharply increases the scope of a study, and second, it is usually difficult to study deviant or problem persons, especially when their deviance is a factor which distinguishes their life-style from that of the researchers. Recent literature has abounded with references to whites studying blacks, middle-class researchers studying lower-class behavior patterns, and the like, and the problems associated with those kinds of research activities.

Consideration of the above information as well as a reading of the responses to related questions led us to try to create a "complexity" variable, since we believed that the complexity of the research might be related to the type of research and methodological procedures followed. Some research is so complex that persons committed to "hard science" will shy away from the task. University-supported persons writing grant proposals are most likely to have the luxury of being able to identify their own research problems, and thus to select and define them in manageable terms. Sociologist Otis Dudley Duncan is said to have remarked to a group of colleagues, "We are not in the business of predicting hurricanes, consequently it is better to do well that which is doable than to take on the impossible." The point is that some evaluation-research studies may not really be "doable," especially as they are described in contract proposals. But since profit-making research corporations more often than academicians need the work, they are more likely to answer the call and sell their available skills.

Initially, we planned for a panel of judges to rate the studies on a scale

---

[3] Deviant persons included delinquents or problem individuals, persons affected by problem individuals, such as families of alcoholics, or persons who are victims of crimes, poverty, and discrimination. Service persons were defined as those who administered service and treatment to the target population set for the action program. Territorial units referred to such phenomena as housing conditions, recreational facilities, or neighborhoods.

of complexity using the proposals submitted to the federal agencies as the basis for making the ratings. Unfortunately, that proved to be unfeasible since, as noted, the various agencies differed so widely in proposal format. Thus we were forced to resort to development of a complexity measure from the available questionnaire data. Acknowledging the limitations of this approach, we constructed a dichotomous variable, complex–less complex, as a limited attempt to examine this issue. Studies were categorized as complex if they (1) were national, regional, or statewide in scope, (2) defined and researched two or more groups as the target populations, (3) focused on groups and organizations as the unit of analysis in addition to single individuals, and (4) were reported by the investigator to be evaluations of programs which are politically controversial. Of the 236 studies, 23 met all four criteria.

There was no significant relationship between a study being categorized as complex and its particular problem focus. However, we did find that studies categorized as complex tended to carry larger budgetary stipends ($100,000 or more), were more often contracts (74 percent) than grants (26 percent), and were likely to have been supported by one of the federal agencies which we have called "operating agencies." While the limitations to the classification are obvious, this information points to the need for future audits to have a direct complexity measure, since it is clearly related to other important factors.

The last variable we examined within this domain had to do with the nature of the theoretical framework which guided the social-action program. We wish to sidestep the argument on whether evaluation research most often should be exploratory or confirmatory in the sense of theory building. The point is that most intervention efforts, whether they are biomedical or social-action programs, need to be grounded in some theoretical framework. Otherwise, there is no basis for comparison with past action efforts or for the refinement and improvement of the one being evaluated. This is not to deny the value of social experimentation, but rather to define it as a means of developing, testing or refining theories of social change. Merton (1949) called attention to the need for theory and research to develop hand in hand, and there is no reason to assume that this dictum is any less imperative for evaluation research.

With respect to theoretical frameworks, there seem to be three distinct patterns in evaluation studies. In the first, a social-action program is derived directly from some explicit theoretical framework. For example, the Mobilization for Youth program was rooted in Cloward and Ohlin's (1961) viewpoint on increasing structural opportunities. In the second, there is no clear conceptual basis for a program, but the evaluator, as a social scientist, casts the evaluation research in some theoretical framework in order to better guide his or her study. Embedding an evaluation in a theoretical framework makes the research effort more similar to traditional "basic" investigations. The third pattern is the most common one, i.e., the action program is not guided by any discernible theoretical framework.

We find that only slightly more than 18 percent (43) of the total studies were evaluating programs reported as having some underlying conceptual or theoretical framework. Some 60 percent were said to be guided by a social-service model, i.e., one which holds that the provision of services is good—for example, that job training benefits the unemployed; and some 16 percent were reported as having no theoretical model at all. This apparent lack of grounding evaluation efforts in some theoretical framework will be particularly important when we later examine levels of methodological adequacy. While our data indicate that the nature of the theoretical framework was not significantly related to either problem focus or complexity, we argue (and later demonstrate) that having an explicit theoretical framework is more characteristic of what we regard as academic rather than entrepreneurial research.

THE EVALUATION RESEARCH ORGANIZATION AND ITS STAFF

One of the most interesting aspects about the state of evaluation research is that little is known about those who do the work. Specifically, we focused upon two dimensions: (1) the nature of the organization with which the evaluator was affiliated, and (2) the background and careers of the investigators.

We know from past studies (Miller 1955; Bello 1956; Ben-David 1960; Kornhauser 1962; Hagstrom 1965; Boalt and Lantz 1970; and Persell 1971) that the organization for which one works shapes, in part, the projects one works on, as well as the way the work is done. Evaluation research, unlike most other research activities, is done by persons of markedly different backgrounds with varied organizational affiliations. Our data show that in fiscal 1970, 27 percent of the awards went to persons in profit-making research corporations; 22 percent to persons in nonprofit research corporations, including nonuniversity research institutes; 34 percent to persons in universities or university-affiliated centers; and 16 percent to persons in public agencies, social service agencies, or social welfare planning units.

In addition to the type of organization, we obtained information regarding geographic location and whether or not the organization had received more than one award for evaluation research in fiscal 1970. We thought it would be interesting to determine if organizations, especially profit-making research corporations, would receive more awards if they were located closer to the funding source, Washington, D.C. Our suspicions were partially confirmed. Of the awards given to profit-making corporations, the highest proportion was located nearest the Washington area. Perhaps, as Biderman and Sharp (1972) suggest, this is due to their deliberate attempt to locate themselves nearer "the action." We also found that 35 percent of the organizations had received more than one award for evaluation that year. However, that figure is somewhat misleading since, in fact, most of the multiple awards went to large organizations and universities, where different groups of researchers were involved in separate awards. Thus there seemed to be no grounds for asserting that in fiscal 1970 any groups had monopolies of awards.

The last dimension examined was the organization's relative prestige or status in the scientific community. Using a judgmental ranking system, we grouped the organizations conducting the studies into high- and low-prestige categories.[4] Of those classified as high prestige, 49 percent were profit corporations and 33 percent were educational institutions. Only 12 percent were nonprofit groups or public agencies. This was not surprising since there are few prestigious nonprofit research corporations and even fewer prestigious public-service agencies.

We also gathered data on four characteristics of the researchers. These were the highest earned academic degree, the years of related work experience, the academic discipline of training, and the major audience to whom the evaluator was addressing himself or herself in writing up the results. A high proportion of evaluators had a doctoral degree (see Figure 3.2); further, most were reportedly experienced researchers with more than ten years in their field (see Figure 3.3). The largest proportion of persons was trained in psychology, followed by those trained in economics (see Figure 3.4). The "other" category is admittedly high but no single group within that category had more than ten persons. Therefore, we have grouped together lawyers, engineers, and so on.

The majority of evaluators do *not* describe their major audience as an academic one (Figure 3.5). That is, they do not intend to publish their results in a monograph or journal and do not regard colleagues and other

---

[4] This measure is based on the subjective judgments of the investigators. In general, high prestige was assigned to the large, national profit-making groups as opposed to the smaller, locally-centered ones. Additionally, to rate the universities, the Cartter Report (1966) was used. While no claims are being made for its reliability and validity, it provided us with a "quick and dirty" estimate of what might be an interesting variable.

Figure 3.2

Highest Degree of Project Director

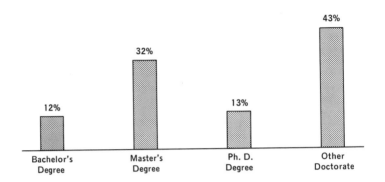

researchers as one of their major constituencies. The major audience is especially interesting to us, since we knew that previous studies (Davis 1954; Meltzer 1956; Pelz 1956; Whyte 1956; Gouldner 1957; Merton 1957; Kornhauser 1962; Cole and Cole 1967; and Persell 1971) have shown that the more academic one's orientation is, the higher the quality of the scientific product.

Of central concern is the interrelationship among these variables: e.g., what kinds of persons are affiliated with what kinds of organizational settings and are there systematic relationships between types of organizations

Figure 3.3

Years of Experience of Project Director

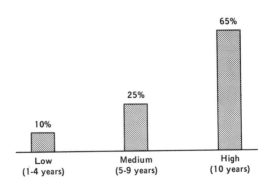

Figure 3.4

Academic Discipline of Project Director

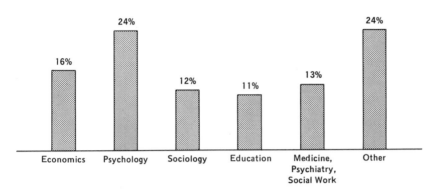

and personnel characteristics? Looking first at the highest earned degree and the type of organization (see Table 3.3) we find that 43 percent of persons whose highest degree is a bachelor's degree are located in profit-making research corporations,[5] whereas the highest proportion of persons with Ph.D.'s (46 percent of the 101 investigators) or other doctorates, e.g.,

Figure 3.5

Major Audience for Project Director

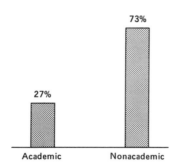

---

[5] Like the "complexity" variable, the "audience" variable was a construct combining responses to several items. While a more comprehensive set of questions would have been better, we did what we could to tap this issue within the constraints posed by the limitations of our data.

Table 3.3. Highest Degree of Project Director and
Type of Organizational Affiliation

	Degree of Project Director			
Type of Organization	$(N = 28)$ B.A.	$(N = 74)$ M.A.	$(N = 30)$ Other Dr.	$(N = 101)$* Ph.D.
Profit	42.9%	37.8%	13.3%	17.8%
Nonprofit	25.0	20.3	23.3	22.8
Educational	10.7	20.3	56.7	45.5
Public-service agency	21.4	21.6	6.7	13.9

$\chi^2 = 31.9$, p $<.001$
* Three cases omitted because of lack of information.

M.D., Ed.D. (57 percent of the 30 researchers), are in educational institutions, e.g., universities.[6] Profit-making research corporations may hire persons without advanced degrees because they cannot attract the more highly degreed individuals, who prefer university environments. At the same time, of course, persons with lower degrees often cannot acquire positions in universities and so they seek jobs in alternative organizations. This relationship between degree and type of organization will be especially important to recall when we discuss levels of methodological adequacy and types of organization.

We do not find any statistically significant relationship between extensiveness of experience and the type of organization with which the investigator is affiliated. We do find, however, that persons of different academic backgrounds are systematically located in certain types of organizations (see Table 3.4). To a large extent, economists are located in profit-making research corporations, whereas psychologists typically are working in university settings. In part, this may reflect the long history of the involvement of economists in governmental and applied-research settings. Psychologists and sociologists have only more recently been recognized as direct contributors to the shaping of public policy, and so they are probably still less likely to stray from the more traditional university setting. Additionally, persons in the fields of psychology and sociology may still have certain misgivings about working on applied research, especially in nonuniversity settings. There probably remains in these fields a residue of disdain for

---

[6] Characteristics of the researcher are based on the responses given about the project director. However, we have data on the principal investigator and person most essential to the execution of the study on a daily basis as well. Since they were so similar and the federal agency often only has information about the project director prior to making the award, we present only data on the project director.

Table 3.4. Academic Discipline and Type of Organizational
Affiliation of Project Director

Type of Organization	Academic Discipline					
	($N=38$) Economics	($N=57$) Psychology	($N=28$) Sociology	($N=30$) Medicine, Social Work, Psychiatry	($N=25$) Education	($N=55$)* Other
Profit	47%	7%	32%	3%	28%	42%
Non-profit	21	23	18	23	20	25
Educational institution	21	49	36	54	28	22
Public-service agency	11	21	14	20	24	11

$\chi^2 = 41.4$, p $<.001$
* Three cases omitted because of lack of information.

the person who leaves the "ivory tower" for a working world where the contribution to scientific knowledge is not always the reigning goal. Economists, especially those without a Ph.D., have a tradition of operating in alternative environments.

Given the findings that evaluators trained in economics and persons without doctoral degrees are more likely to be found in profit-making research corporations and psychologists and persons with doctoral degrees are more likely to be found in educational institutions, we attempted to determine further if their definition of purpose varies as well. Using the variable discussed earlier, "major audience," we first examined whether or not investigators in different types of organizations have different audiences. Blau (1955), Gouldner (1957), Lazarsfeld and Thielens (1958), Kornhauser (1962), and Hagstrom (1965) all note that persons working in universities tend to be more committed to communicating with an academic audience than persons working in government laboratories, service institutions, industry, or other nonuniversity organizations. Our data confirms this view. Of those evaluators who defined their audience as academic (63), 50 percent were affiliated with educational institutions. In Table 3.5 we show that evaluators in educational institutions, nonprofit research corporations, and public service planning agencies all are more likely to define their orientation as academic than those in profit-making research corporations. This suggests, then, that perhaps the profit motive and its accompanying normative system take precedence over traditional scientific norms, with the result that evaluators in profit corporations define some other audience as the major group with which they wish to communicate.

Table 3.5. Percent of Investigators Defining Major Audience as Academic

Type of Organization	Percent	100% equals
Profit making	6%	64
Public Service Planning	24	38
Nonprofit making	34	53
Educational	40	81

$\chi^2 = 22.0$, p $<.001$

Since the type of organization is systematically related to the definition of one's major audience, and since we had already established that certain types of researchers are found in certain types of organizations, we assumed that the characteristics of the researcher might influence the definition of a major audience. After all, part of the training one receives when pursuing an advanced degree is said to involve an internalization of the norm which asserts that one's colleagues are always the most important audience (Hagstrom 1965). In support of this idea, we find that evaluators with doctoral degrees (37 percent) are much more likely to define their audience as academic than are those without doctoral degrees; additionally, we find that psychologists (37 percent) and persons in medicine or social work (43 percent) are more likely to define their audience as academic than are

Table 3.6. Percent of Project Directors Oriented to Academic
Audience by Type of Organization, Degree, and Discipline

	Organization							
	Profit Making				Nonprofit Making			
	No Doctorate		Doctorate		No Doctorate		Doctorate	
Discipline	Percent	100% equals	Percent	100% equals	Percent	100% equals	Percent	100% equals
Economics	—	(12)	—	(6)	—	(9)	18%	(11)
Psychology	—	(2)	—	(2)	11%	(9)	45	(44)
Sociology	—	(5)	—	(4)	33	(6)	38	(13)
Education	25%	(4)	—	(3)	17	(6)	42	(12)
Medicine, Psychiatry, Social work	—	(—)	100%	(1)	36	(11)	44	(18)
Other	12	(17)	—	(6)	19	(21)	64	(11)

economists (5 percent). Of course, many of the economists in our study were persons whose highest degree was a bachelor's degree and who often were working in nonuniversity settings as compared to the psychologists in our sample who almost all had Ph.D. degrees and were mostly working out of a university-based research center.

Clearly, the characteristics of the evaluation-research unit and the investigators are systematically related to one another. A simple diagram based on the four major dimensions is shown in Figure 3.6. There are two major discernible patterns. The first seems to be that typically the evaluator in the profit-making corporation is a person who has a bachelor's degree either in economics or in a "social-science related field," e.g., public affairs, and does not define his or her *major* audience as academic. The almost opposite pattern is that of the evaluator who works in an educational institution, has a doctoral degree in a social science field or medicine, and defines his or her major audience as academic. As before, these two model types clearly are not all inclusive, but for our purposes they pinpoint patterns of relationships among key dimensions. They are especially important because our later examination of methodological adequacy will show that one pattern seems to be conducive to a more adequate scientific product than the other.

Figure 3.6

Characteristics of the Evaluation Research Unit

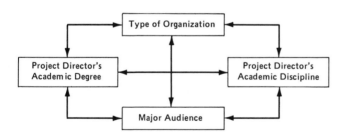

Having described the way in which evaluation-research awards are given, their purpose, the scope which they cover, and the personnel and organizations who receive those awards, the question next raised is, "How are they carried out?" The act and the actors have been defined, but the process by which they relate to one another has yet to be elaborated. Specifically, we turn next to a brief look at who makes the decisions about ways in which the evaluation should be carried out. Toward that end we turn to a discussion of our fourth and final descriptive set of measures—the interorganizational network.

CHARACTERISTICS OF THE
INTERORGANIZATIONAL NETWORK

In Chapter 1, we noted that the organizational arrangements which define the evaluation-research enterprise run from almost total independence to almost total interdependence with respect to the ways in which the funding (sponsoring) agency and the social-action agency formally and informally relate to the evaluation staff. In order to sort out some of the entanglements posed by these varied interorganizational networks, we included questions about (1) the formal organizational arrangements between the evaluation and action staffs, (2) the working relationship between the evaluation staff and action-program staff with respect to decisions about the research procedures, and (3) the working relationship between the evaluation staff and funding-agency staff with respect to decisions about research procedures. These three dimensions were of special interest to us not only for descriptive purposes, but also because the evaluation-research literature is replete with references to the political and methodological implications of these varied arrangements. Argyris (1958), Downs (1965), Freeman and Sherwood (1965) and Weiss (1971) are but a few who have discussed the influence practitioners and policy persons have on researchers in evaluation settings.

The first measure, on the formal organizational arrangements between the evaluation staff and the action staff, provides data on the "insider-outsider" question. We found that in 38 percent of the investigations, the same organization conducted *both* the action program and evaluation research; in 42 percent the evaluation and action components were partly or completely conducted by different organizations; in 12 percent the evaluation and action components were conducted by different organizations where one was a subcontractor of the other; and in 8 percent the evaluation and action components were both subcontractors of a third organization. Adding these last three groups together, we find that 62 percent of the evaluations were conducted by organizations different, at least in part, from the groups conducting the action program. One further piece of information is that of the 38 percent ($N = 90$) in which the action and evaluation efforts were conducted by the same organization, only 25 percent ($N = 23$) had the same persons doing both tasks. Most often, these groups tended to either share some common staff (49 percent) or have totally different staffs (26 percent). Again, this will be important to consider when we examine the levels of relative methodological adequacy of the research and how it relates to the various types of organizational arrangements.

The second variable focuses on the working relationship between the action program and evaluation research staffs regarding the making of research decisions. This issue is a source of debate. The most frequent assertion is that the more closely related the action and evaluation staffs are in terms of working relationships, the greater the likelihood that the researcher's commitment to rigorous research procedures would be hindered by a commitment to service and the continued longevity of the program. The most serious implication is that the evaluator would supposedly opt for a "softer" evaluation which would allow for greater flexibility in interpretation of findings rather than face the consequences of negative findings which would endanger the continuance of the program. (Caro [1971] provides a comprehensive review of this debate.)

The converse assertion is that if the evaluation staff largely works *independent* of the action staff, rather than interdependently with them, they run the risk of falling prey to all the functional problems which besiege organizational research settings when personnel of divergent value orientations attempt to operate in the same locale. There is a litany of complaints and consequences of practitioner-versus-researcher type arrangements: evaluators have been accused of stealing precious resources from the needy and the disadvantaged, denying human services for the sake of having a control group and earning their living by "chopping others down." Consequently, the often-cited result is that the action staff defends itself by thwarting the evaluator in his or her research procedures, and by denying him or her the use of control groups, access to records, and so on.

Much of the literature suggests that, on the one hand, those who work *interdependently* often are co-opted by the program people and compromise the quality of their research in an effort to live in harmony with the action staff. On the other hand, it often is held that evaluation investigators who work *independently* of the action staff lose access to data and subjects and thus the quality of their research is compromised. It is suggested then that in either case the evaluator is involved in a "can't-win" situation. Our own estimation of the association between the kind of working relationship one has and research quality is presented in the following chapters. For the time being, we shall examine the distribution of responses on this variable among the studies in our study group.

We find that 40 percent ($N = 100$) of our study group report that they work interdependently or jointly with one another, i.e., research decisions about the evaluation study are made as a result of cooperative efforts of the evaluation and action staffs. Nineteen percent ($N = 45$) replied they operate more independently; that is, the conduct of the evaluation research is determined primarily by the evaluators but formally reviewed by the action-program staff. The remaining 39 percent ($N = 91$) say they work independent of the action staff, and the relationship between the two groups, if any, is confined to fiscal and related administrative decisions.

As one might expect, the type of working relationship is closely associated with organizational arrangements. Joint planning for research decisions occurred most often when the evaluation and action staffs worked within the same organizational framework (see Table 3.7). An example

Table 3.7. Working Relationships between Research and Action Groups

Working Relationship	Organizational Arrangements	
	($N = 90$) Same Organization	($N = 146$) Different Organization
Joint planning	80%	19%
Action reviews evaluator's decisions	6	27
Evaluation staff independent	14	54

$\chi^2 = 84.5$, p $< .001$

of this somewhat common occurrence—i.e., the evaluation and action staffs are part of the same organization and there is joint planning—was an evaluation of a community mental-health center. The research and action-program staffs were located in different wings of the same neighborhood mental-health clinic. While different persons administered the service and research operations separately, they worked together closely in making decisions about the research design and how it would be implemented. The service group served as a natural laboratory for the researcher and his findings served as the basis for feedback and program modification. Interestingly, the process was deemed appropriate and beneficial by both parties.

The third variable studied in this set was the working relationship between the evaluation staff and sponsoring-agency staff with respect to the making of research decisions. Coleman (1971) is especially insightful about the value conflicts which exist between the funding-agency staff and the evaluators, particularly when the latter align themselves professionally with a scientific discipline. For our purposes, the relevant point of his paper is that sponsoring agencies require rapid feedback about complex problems and programs and have only limited time and money in order to secure the information they require. As such, policy persons are not oriented toward massive data collection and analysis as is often required by investigators before they feel comfortable enough to make suggested policy statements based on their research. The different value orientations and needs often give rise to divergent priorities and expectations about how the research should be carried out.

In only 7 percent of the studies reviewed, research decisions about evaluation designs were made by the funding-agency staff, not the evaluation staff; in 18 percent, decisions about the research design were made jointly by evaluation and funding-agency staffs; in 34 percent, the research decisions were made primarily by the evaluation staff but reviewed by the funding-agency staff; and in 42 percent, research decisions were made solely by the evaluation staff.

Our data indicate that these three variables are systematically associated with one another. In terms of organizational arrangements, as shown in Table 3.8, when the evaluation and action staffs are both under the roof

Table 3.8. Working Relationship between Evaluation and Funding Groups

Working Relationship	Research-Action Organizational Arrangements	
	$(N = 89)$ Same Organization	$(N = 144)*$ Different Organization
Funding makes decisions	6%	8%
Joint planning	5	26
Funding reviews decisions	32	35
Evaluation staff independent	58	31

$\chi^2 = 24.4$, p $<.001$
* Three cases omitted because of lack of information.

of the same organization, there is a greater tendency for the evaluators to be independent of the funding staff. Perhaps this is due to the fact that funding agencies may feel a need for closer control over the evaluation when the evaluation staff and action staff are not working interdependently, and that the funding group can mediate difficulties which may arise. Note, in Table 3.8, that when the evaluation and action staffs are independent of one another, i.e., in different organizations, there is a greater tendency for the evaluation and funding staff to work more closely together ("joint planning").

The association between the variable "working relationship between evaluation and action" and "working relationship between evaluation and funding" shows the same, albeit weaker pattern. That is, as one might expect, given the results of Table 3.8, when the action and evaluation staffs make joint decisions about the research, they tend not to consult with the funding agency. In other words, when the evaluation and action staffs work interdependently with one another, they are more independent of the funding agency. Two other interesting points are: first, when the evaluation team has the action staff review the research decisions, they also tend to have the funding staff review the decisions; second, when the evaluation staff makes research decisions independent of the action staff there appears to be a tendency to also make decisions independent of the funding staff (Table 3.9).

Table 3.9. Working Relationship between the Evaluation and Action Staffs and the Working Relationship between the Evaluation and Funding Staffs

Working Relationship between Evaluation and Funding Staffs	Working Relationship between Evaluation and Action Staffs		
	$(N = 99)$ Joint Planning	$(N = 45)$ Formal Review by Action over Eval.	$(N = 89)$* Eval. Work Independently
Funding makes research decisions	9%	5%	6%
Joint planning between eval. and fund.	15	22	18
Eval. research decisions reviewed by fund.	29	53	29
Eval. makes research decisions independently	47	20	47

$\chi^2 = 14.7, p < .05$
* Three cases omitted because of lack of information.

Some examples of this can be cited: a study evaluating the effectiveness of a cognitive development program for preschool children had its action and evaluation components conducted within the same organization. However, these efforts were undertaken by different persons. The research decisions concerning the design for the evaluation were made jointly with the action staff by the evaluators but independent of the funding-agency staff except for periodic formal reviews. This evaluation was an NIH-sponsored grant to a university-based research group.

In another evaluation, this one funded as a contract by OEO to evaluate the effectiveness of a program (which shall remain unnamed to preserve anonymity), we find that the evaluation and action components were conducted by different organizations where one was a subcontractor of the other. With respect to decisions about the evaluation-research design, the action and evaluation staffs worked independently of one another. When asked to characterize the relationship to the funding agency, the evaluator's response was "poor, confused—we did the evaluation, they reviewed the results," indicating for our purposes that they operated largely independently of the funding agency as well. We cite this example because evaluators who work independent from both action and funding staffs will be interesting later when we examine methodological quality.

We can specify further the patterns these relationships take. Table 3.10 is a presentation of the three variables and Figure 3.7 gives a pictorial representation of them.

Table 3.10. Working Relationship between Evaluation, Action, and Funding Groups

| | Between Evaluation and Action Groups | | | |
| | (N = 89) Same Organization | | (N = 144) Different Organization | |
Between Evaluation and Funding Groups	(N = 71) Joint	(N = 18) Separate	(N = 28) Joint	(N = 116)* Separate
Evaluation and Funding, joint	11%	5%	57%	29%
Evaluation and Funding, separate	89	95	43	72

* Three cases omitted because of lack of information.

Figure 3.7

Characteristics of the Interorganizational Network

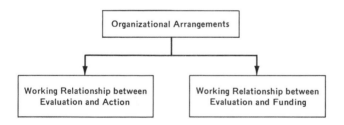

The interorganizational network produces three discernible patterns of association. The first occurs when the evaluation is conducted by the organization administering the social-action program. The predominant pattern is for the evaluators to work *independently* of the funding-agency staff and

interdependently with the action-agency staff with respect to research decisions. When, however, the action and evaluation components are conducted partly or completely in different organizations, there is some evidence to suggest that, especially for those who work jointly with the action staff, joint decision-making with the funding-agency staff is undertaken as well. The third pattern is one in which the evaluators are organizationally separated from the action program and work independent of both the action-program staff and the funding-agency staff.

ACADEMICS AND ENTREPRENEURS

We have presented in the preceding pages an overview of the characteristics which define the state of the art of evaluation research. Our presentation has, however, been confined to key dimensions which fell into specified content areas, and to how the dimensions in each domain relate to one another. We have hinted at the fact that many of the variables in different areas are systematically related to variables in other areas, e.g., the use of a theoretical framework is related to the evaluator's academic discipline; evaluations guided by a formal theory have a greater likelihood of having a project director who is trained in psychology. Without systematically discussing all of the relationships of each variable with every other one, which would necessitate a discussion of some 300 cross-tabulations, we can present two extreme types or styles of evaluation activity. These types are a means of highlighting predominant patterns of association, and only a few actual cases will correspond exactly to the model.[7] (Appendix III is a matrix of the chi-square tests of significance for the association of each variable with every other variable for further perusal.)

The first type—which we refer to as the *academic*—typifies the characteristics associated with *grants* awarded by research-oriented federal agencies, such as NIMH and NIH. These grants, by the nature of the funding agencies involved, tend to be awarded for evaluations focusing on programs aimed at ameliorating health and mental-health problems. They are likely to be studies with relatively small budgets. Further, they are likely to last two years or more.

These research-oriented agencies rely heavily upon the peer-review system and on a fairly open competition in the award decision-making process. They allocate the majority of their awards to academicians since they are likely to have the strongest records in terms of indicators of scien-

---

[7] For a discussion of the advantages of the use of typologies or models in research, see Bailey (1973), especially the section on typologies wherein he asserts that they serve to highlight the predominant patterns of association without explicitly showing the internal variation within the parts of the model by individual cases.

tific productivity and promise—e.g., publications in refereed journals. Moreover, peer reviewers use productivity as one criterion for making the award. Also, most of the peer reviewers are university-based themselves and probably have a bias for others with this affiliation. Since academicians are receiving most of these awards, they are likely to hold doctoral degrees, given the requirements for academic positions. In addition, while not all of this group of evaluators define their major audience as academic, and not all are evaluating a program which is guided by some formal theoretical framework, the proportion in both cases is high. University-based academicians, who predominate among persons in this type, usually embrace the most basic "discipline norms" that one should disseminate research in scholarly journals or monographs, and that the academic community affords greatest prestige to knowledge which makes a contribution to theory (Merton 1957, Caplow and McGee 1958; and Hagstrom 1965). It is interesting that these characteristics are not unlike the patterns one would find if one were examining grant support of more "basic research" by these same agencies. In fact, we note that the patterns remain almost identical, despite the fact that evaluation research is being supported and is characteristically defined as "applied or policy-related research."

Concluding our discussion of this type, we cite the three case examples in Table 3.11. One of the cases was specifically chosen to represent a variation of the model to emphasize that there is internal variation within the polar types we have set up.

The *entrepreneurial type* is almost the polar opposite of the academic, typifying the conditions associated with contracts supported usually by "operating agencies," e.g., Department of Labor, HUD, or the OEO. These agencies, as mainly service-oriented branches of the government, tend to award mostly contracts, because the evaluations they support usually arise in response to a felt need to make a policy decision about some social-action program they also support or have promoted. For example, the now famous Head Start program was first sponsored by OEO and first evaluated under its auspices as well. Unlike the academic type, the entrepreneurial type usually includes studies with larger budgets but relatively shorter time spans. Since they are contracts and thus often put out on a "Request for Proposal" (RFP) basis, the time schedule is tight. As such, it is not difficult to understand why academicians are usually not equipped to answer these RFP's. Their schedules are less flexible, and they often prefer not to work on research that is highly structured in terms of time, budgetary allotment, and sometimes even design procedures. Moreover, some federal agencies may be wary of awarding contracts to academicians because of the latters' reputation of unconcern with temporal and budgetary priorities. A federal agency administrator said: "The reason we give our money to profit-mak-

Table 3.11. Case Examples of Academic Studies

Case Examples	A	B	C
Sponsoring agency and nature of award	NIH grant	NIMH grant	SRS grant
Focus of action program	Health and education	Mental health	Income security
Budget for evaluation research	$70,000	$75,905	$394,812
Length of time for study (extensions not included)	2 years	2 years, 3 months	2 years
Type of organization evaluator is affiliated with	University	University	University
Highest degree of project director	Ph.D.	Ph.D.	Ph.D.
Academic discipline of project director	Psychology	Psychology	Sociology
Years of relevant experience of project director	20	10	10
Major audience for findings	Academic	Academic	Nonacademic
Theory guiding action program	Social-psychological theory	Social-psychological theory	Social-structural theory

Case A was an evaluation of the effects (short and long term) of an intervention program aimed at improving the cognitive functioning of preschool children from a minority group in society.

Case B was an evaluation of the effects of innovative counseling programs made available to students on college campuses for the purposes of bettering mental-health services.

Case C was an evaluation of the effects of a graduated family allowance income maintenance program aimed at the poor and near-poor in a selected model-cities area.

ing corporations is because we know they won't exceed the budget and we know they'll hand in the report on time." In addition to the fact that profit-making corporations are equipped to bid for contracts, they also seem to resent less the "involuntary" selection of the problem. Perhaps this results from the fact that they tend more to see themselves in part as serving the government rather than feeling that the government should exist to support their research. In any case, the result is that awards made as contracts go most often to profit corporations. Further, since profit corporations are less prestigious as organizational bases, and less typically ideal career pathways for investigators, at least for persons from medicine, psychology, and sociology, it is not surprising that they usually employ persons with less advanced degrees. It is important to note that the economists in our study largely did not have Ph.D. degrees but rather held only bachelor's degrees.

Project directors of studies falling within the entrepreneurial type are less likely to define their major audience as academic, or to evaluate programs guided by some theoretical framework. Since profit-making corpora-

Table 3.12. Case Examples of Entrepreneurial Type

Case Examples	D	E	F
Sponsoring agency and nature of award	Labor contract	OEO contract	Labor contract
Focus of action program	Manpower training	Delinquency and income security	Manpower training and education
Budget for evaluation research	$10,000	$300,000	$76,000
Length of time for study (extensions not included)	1 year	1 year, 3 months	7 months
Type of organization evaluator is affiliated with	Profit corporation	Profit corporation	Public service department
Highest degree of project director	M.A.	M.A.	B.A.
Academic discipline of project director	Psychology	Economics	Economics
Years of relevant experience of project director	6	12	13
Major audience for findings	Nonacademic	Nonacademic	Nonacademic
Theory guiding action program	No theory or guiding perspective	No theory or guiding perspective	Social-service model

Case D was an evaluation of the impact of consumer education on reducing unemployment.

Case E was an evaluation of the effectiveness of raising the socioeconomic status of poor youths.

Case F was an evaluation of a program which gave training to state governors for the purpose of aiding them in the development of comprehensive manpower planning.

tions are serving the federal government, they would perhaps be more prone to define their sponsors as a major audience to whom findings are addressed; such positive impressions made upon government groups may lead to receiving more contracts. Similarly, since they are "in business," they can less afford to turn down evaluations on the grounds that the research will not make a theoretical contribution. Since there is no strong norm, as there is in the university, to make a scholarly contribution, they may proceed to undertake evaluations that use a social-service model or no theoretical framework at all.

We present in Table 3.12 a set of case examples of studies which approximate the entrepreneurial type. The two sets of studies highlight the differences.

This ends the description of the research endeavors surveyed. How representative this picture drawn from fiscal year 1970 is of evaluation research in other years is uncertain, but we have no reason to expect that there are great differences, since there have been no major shifts in federal policy and planning. Evaluation research as an industry, an enterprise, or a social phenomenon, involves a set of relationships where one dimension affects another and where there is a high degree of systematic association. We have tried to abstract some general patterns and to present them as concrete types. In doing so, it bears emphasis that we in our use of academic and entrepreneurial types, are referring to more than the orientation, training, and careers of investigators. Rather, they are descriptive of relations between sponsors and investigators and the character of the affiliation of the researcher, as well as his or her own properties (see Chart 3.1).

CHART 3.1

Characteristics of Research Endeavors

Type

	Academic	Entrepreneurial
Funding Agency	Has the support of research as a predominant part of its mission; staff involved in research activities, including planning, negotiations, and monitoring of awards; staff made up of persons with social science and related training and experience.	Primarily concerned with operational programs; staff tends to be dominated by persons with administrative and program experience. Staff engaged in planning, negotiations, and monitoring of awards generally do not have advanced training

Academic	Entrepreneurial

	Academic	Entrepreneurial
	View researchers as colleagues, and funding staff have academic persons as their reference group. Agency staff often identify themselves as members of particular social science disciplines, belong to and attend meetings of social science associations, and sometimes are engaged in own research and publication activities.	and research experience themselves. View researchers as contractors and emphasize the importance of conforming to award specifications including submission of reports on time, performance consistent with specifications, and so on. Tend to identify themselves as professional employees within the federal establishment rather than as persons who have a disciplinary reference group.
Award Process	Awards are grants that have been judged by peer-review groups of persons affiliated with academic-type organizations. Awards are made in competition with other proposals in the same area which have different problem foci. Proposals are initiated by investigators who are often interested in carrying out their line of research for extended periods. Peer judges and agency staff often have personal knowledge of investigator and his (her) organization and technical expertise to judge past work and design aspects of proposals. Investigators submit proposals to meet deadlines three or four times a year, time to develop proposals is often	Awards are contracts provided to organization or individual after competition to undertake advertised need for research contractor. Competition is between potential contractors who have submitted proposals to undertake a specified piece of work. Specifications usually include requirements regarding time period of study. Agency personnel have much more participation and influence in decision-making about who receives support. Often lack technical expertise to judge past work and design of proposal, which may require use of outside consultants. Usually contractors have short period between advertisement of proposal and

	Academic	Entrepreneurial
	lengthy, and the award process takes from six months to one year.	submission of data for consideration. Overall award process short.
Elements in Study	Generally study has formulated frame of reference and theoretical underpinnings. Studies tend to deal with more specified, less complex designs by sites investigated, populations studied, and so on. Generally studies are for extended periods of time, usually two years or more. Most studies include graduate student assistants while the investigator is engaged in personal writing and teaching and spends only part-time on project. Studies generally are under $100,000.	Generally study is developed in ways consistent with an advertised set of specifications. Likely to have been developed in response to legislation or the pressures from Congressmen or executive department administrators and policymakers. More likely to test "service model" idea than theoretical notion. Studies tend to be more complex because of the action programs being evaluated. Most studies represent the major time commitments of the investigator; infrequent use of graduate students and more frequent use of regular technical staff. Studies are large in budget, short in time for completion.
Research Organization	Generally part of university although may be independent nonprofit organization devoted to social research. Activity is seen as furthering the research interests of investigator and colleagues and supplementing and supporting educational program of institution.	Generally a profit-making group. Some are small and with relatively short life spans and low volume of research. Others are large and do consulting and advising for government and industry as well. Activities are oriented to maintenance and expansion of organization and toward profit-making.

	Academic	Entrepreneurial
Research Investigator	Usually a Ph.D., most often in psychology although sociologists are also common. Investigator's career trajectory is academic.	Usually a non-Ph.D. Quite frequently a person with limited graduate training in economics or other related social science disciplines. Careers generally are in nonuniversity-type organizations.
Monitoring and Reporting	Investigator given wide latitude by funding agency. Generally flexible in time extensions, modification of research design, and so on. Only fiscal auditing, with final reports more often than not a formality. Encourages publications in journals and public reporting via monographs and funding-agency publications. Decisions on conduct of research usually made independent of funding agency.	Investigators often have specified reporting requirements. Limited flexibility in time extensions, modification of time specifications, and so on. In addition to fiscal auditing, program reports often required for payments to support research. Generally final report is regarded as the "product." Limited encouragement for professional publication which may require funding-agency permission. Decisions on conduct of research may require participation of funding agency.
Audience	Peers in research and academia are seen as a major audience.	Funding agency and sometimes program personnel are seen as primary audience.

CHAPTER FOUR

Measurement of Process in Evaluation Research

It is our contention, as discussed in Chapter 1, that evaluation-research efforts should contain procedures to measure process if the evaluation of a social-action program or intervention is to be comprehensive and have utility. Hyman and Wright (1967, p. 744) underscore this by stating, "Taking the work for the deed, an evaluator may try to observe the effects of non-existent treatment, or a treatment very different from the one he thought was being examined." A noteworthy case of this kind was made famous by the same two authors, who recount the tale of the evaluation of a propaganda campaign based on the distribution of flyers. After concluding that the distribution of flyers had no significant impact, it was discovered some time later that in fact they had never been distributed. Taking heed from this tale, we are strongly convinced that almost all evaluation research should include the measurement of process. The first step then is to consider in what proportion of studies process was measured.

HOW OFTEN IS PROCESS MEASURED?

Of the 236 evaluations on which we have data, 22 percent (N = 51) reported that the studies *did not* include the measurement of process, i.e., whether or not the program had been implemented according to stated guidelines. This failure to measure process seems to be almost random. None of the twenty-five independent variables discussed in Chapter 3, on which we have data that describe the characteristics of the evaluation-research enterprise, were significantly related to whether or not the study included a measure of process. While this surprised us, both cross-tabular and correlational analysis revealed only three items somewhat systematically related to undertaking or not undertaking a process evaluation; those three were not statistically significant. The first of these three findings was that the shorter the time span of a study, the less likely it was that the evaluation included measures of process. Similarly, projects directed by persons with master's degrees were somewhat less likely to include the measurement of process. While the first finding makes sense in terms of setting priorities for limited time schedules, the second one is harder to understand, since the pattern did not hold for persons with bachelor's degrees, who conduct process analysis as often as persons with doctorates. Thus, it apparently cannot be attributed to a lack of advanced training. Finally, there was an indication that *not* measuring process occurred more often when the evaluation and action components were located in separate organizations (71 percent) rather than in the same organization (29 percent). This is surprising since the reverse would be more understandable; that is, the "inside" evaluator could more naturally make assumptions about the program having been appropriately implemented than the "outside" evaluator.

Although it is only a speculation, we suspect that the failure to find correlates of undertaking or not undertaking a process assessment as part of an evaluation is related to the interaction of different influences. The decision to measure process or not is associated first with a demand from the sponsoring agency to do so; second, with the judgment of the investigator that time, resources, and design possibilities make it feasible to undertake process measurement; and third, with the investigator's judgment that the cooperation of the action group makes it practicable. On the one hand, some evaluations may include process measure on the insistence of the financial sponsor even if measurement of process is regarded as very difficult or impossible; on the other hand, when there is no insistence by the funding agency, either wise judgment on the part of the investigator or lack of concern with making a comprehensive evaluation may be related to not measuring process. In other words, the decision to measure or not may, from the standpoint of sound social research, be a wise or unwise one, depending on the individual set of circumstances. Clearly, in designing this audit of evaluation research, we did not think through entirely the issues involved, and accordingly do not have the data necessary to substantiate this view.

APPROACHES TO MEASURING PROCESS

The information we collected on methodological procedures to measure process centered on four standard research concerns. The first is the *methods used in the collection of data.* We were interested in determining the specific methods used, the sources of information, and the structured or unstructured nature of the information. We do not believe that one method or data source is better or worse than another; rather, the information will be treated as indicative of the "state of the art."

Our second concern was with *sampling procedures,* and here the findings can be judged along a dimension of greater or lesser quality. That is, most persons concerned with research methodology hold that representative sampling is an essential part of all scientific procedures (Goode and Hatt 1952, p. 210). Adequate sampling procedures help rule out biased findings, certainly a recurring problem in evaluation research (Williams and Evans 1969). Thus, we were concerned with the type of sampling procedures used by the evaluator.

The third procedure dealt with the *data analytic techniques* used, again both for the sake of describing what was done and to be able to judge the quality of work. Our position here is more controversial. In judging quality, we have taken the view that multivariate techniques are better than less sophisticated analytic approaches. Admittedly not all social scientists will agree that the use of sophisticated analytic techniques are "better" in demonstrable ways, but certainly most believe that they allow for more thorough and definitive mining of data. This is not to suggest that elegance is always superior to simplicity, but rather that, in general, evaluation-research efforts can be enhanced by the use of the most sophisticated techniques available.

The fourth measure of process we observed was concerned with the *nature of the analysis,* i.e., whether it was *quantitative, qualitative* or about *evenly divided.* While this variable clearly is related to the previous one, it differs in the sense that it represents an overview of the research process as a whole, and the evaluator's self-report about how best to characterize his or her efforts. To cast a research effort as quantitative implies more than the mere use of multivariate statistics. It implies the acceptance of a set of assumptions and directions about how research should proceed and how data should be interpreted. It is our contention that quantitative analyses are better suited to the needs of evaluation research than qualitative ones.

Again, while for some this is a debatable issue, it would seem that it really is a decision based on trade-offs. If one uses quantitative methods and procedures, one assumes that there is some regularity about the phenomenon being studied and that reducing the characteristics to numerical categories will not destroy the value of the data. In quantitative analysis, data are grouped on the basis of similarities. There often is a cost, namely the loss of uniqueness. But insofar as policy-makers are interested in the general conditions associated with successful program implementation and impact rather than particular unique successes, the use of quantitative methods is more likely to allow the mustering of strong empirical evidence to support wide-reaching decisions. Additionally, most social-action programs are aimed at large numbers of persons, and this too argues for the use of quantitative methods since they permit ordering of large amounts of information about numerous people. In quantitative analyses one loses the richer, more in-depth kind of picture that emerges from qualitative analyses, but given the needs of evaluation research, we contend that in most cases the use of quantitative methods is best suited to the task. Accordingly, in addition to describing the fundamental analytical approach, it reflects more often than not the quality of the study.

Methods of Data Collection

As indicated in our introductory remarks, we were interested in determining the methods used in the collection of data, primarily for descriptive purposes. We organized the reported sources of data into two groups. One set of data sources did not require direct contact with informants. That is, either by direct observation or by use of action-agency records and reports, it was possible to complete data on the way programs were undertaken. The second type of information required direct contact with either the recipients of programs or with service personnel or other community members knowledgeable about them.

Agency records were the dominant source of data used to assess implementation, with four-fifths of the 185 studies in which process measurement occurred making use of this data source. The other three approaches—observations, information obtained directly from clients or persons in the target population, and information from service personnel or knowledgeable community members—were each used in almost 70 percent of the studies. Thus, it is clear that when process was measured, multiple sources were tapped. Over 50 percent of the studies used information obtained both directly from clients and from either observation or records. Indeed, in about one-third of the 185 studies in which process was measured, at least three different methods of data collection were employed (see Figure 4.1).

Sampling

Earlier we indicated that we would order the sampling procedures undertaken going from those most to those least recommended and appropriate on the basis of traditional views on strengths and weaknesses of various sampling methods. Using Blalock's (1972) definitions of sampling, simple random, stratified random, and cluster were employed as categories. Two additional categories were used: "systematic nonrandom" sampling

Figure 4.1

Sources of Data

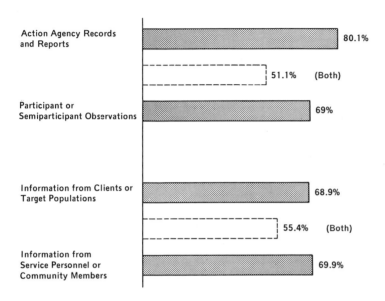

refers to selection that was not random but where there was some attempt made to be systematic. For example, in the case of the evaluation of a corrections program, those inmates who had entered prison on the first of the month were selected for interviews. This method is systematic but clearly not random. There seems to be no justification for the first of the month other than the fact that it was convenient. The last category, "nonsystematic, nonrandom" refers to evaluations in which units were selected for study on an arbitrary or opportunistic basis. In one study, for example, the evaluator indicated the sample was selected on the basis of "persons available and willing to talk." Similarly, another evaluation assessed process by conducting informal discussions with volunteers who had participated in the welfare-reform program. These last two categories represent the use of procedures which are not generally regarded as sound. Figure 4.2 shows the distribution on this variable, grouped into three judgmental categories.

Examining the 185 studies that included process analyses we find that 36 percent used something less than the recommended procedures. One of the tasks of evaluations is to provide unbiased and hopefully generalizable information; inadequate sampling may result in erroneous conclusions.

Given the wide variation in sampling procedures, and the fact that

Figure 4.2

Distribution of Sampling Procedures as Used in the Measurement of Process

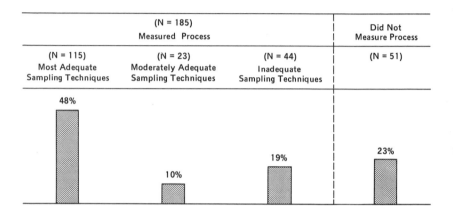

---

* *Most Adequate* is composed of the 88 evaluations that observed or examined all the
units that were targets of the action program, 13 that used a simple random sample, and
14 that used a stratified random sample.
Moderately Adequate represents those 23 that used a cluster sample.
Inadequate represents the 25 which used systematic nonrandom techniques and the 19
which used nonsystematic nonrandom techniques.

some evaluations used more highly regarded procedures than others, we
tried to identify correlates of the use of different procedures. In Table 4.1,
we present variables significantly associated (at the $p < .05$ level or better)
with the variable "sampling procedures," when these are grouped as described in Figure 4.2. Interesting results occur, especially given our presentation of the academic and entrepreneurial types discussed in Chapter 3.
The nature of the award, the training of the investigators, and the relations
between the evaluators and their sponsors and the action group, distinguish
those who used what we regard as either sound or questionable sampling
procedures. The use of recommended sampling procedures was most common among academic types whereas the highest proportion of studies using
less adequate techniques was drawn from those resembling the entrepreneurial type. The correlates of evaluation studies in which the most adequate sampling techniques were used in the measurement of process appear
to be: grants, evaluations conducted as awards funded by research-oriented
agencies, awards for longer durations of time, awards made to projects
where the director held a doctoral degree, awards where the evaluation and

Table 4.1. Summary Table of Variables Statistically Associated (p<.05) with the Various Sampling Procedures

| | Sampling Procedures* | |
Variables	(N = 138) Of Those Evaluators Using Moderately Adequate or Better Techniques (all observed, random, or cluster samples)	(N = 44) Of Those Evaluators Using Inadequate Techniques (systematic nonrandom, or nonsystematic nonrandom)
Nature of the award	38% were contracts 62% were grants	64% were contracts 36% were grants
Sponsoring agency†	36% OE, other HEW, Agriculture, Labor, HUD, and OEO 64% NIH, NIMH, SRS, and Justice	55% OE, other HEW, HUD, Agriculture, Labor, and OEO 45% NIH, NIMH, SRS, and Justice
Length of study	30% 18 months 70% 18 months	46% 18 months 54% 18 months
Degree of project director	65% doctorates 35% not doctorates	54% doctorates 46% not doctorates
Organizational arrangements between evaluation and action staffs	46% evaluation and action same organization 54% evaluation and action different organization	25% evaluation and action same organization 75% evaluation and action different organization
Working relationship between evaluation and action staffs‡	33% evaluation and action staffs work independently 67% evaluation and action staffs work interdependently	46% evaluation and action staff work independently 54% evaluation and action staff work interdependently

* This table is based on the 185 evaluations that included measures of process. Percentages are calculated along the dependent variable in order to summarize the information.

‡ Independent means that the evaluation staff made the decisions about the research without consultation or review by the action-program staff.

† In this table the various agencies are grouped together based on their similarities in functions and operations. However, tables in the following chapters show differences among each agency as well.

action staffs were formally part of the same organization, and those where the evaluation and action staffs make decisions about the research interdependently. Conversely, in evaluations using less adequate sampling procedures, there was a greater likelihood that they were contracts, awards given by "operating agencies," awards for shorter time spans, awards where the evaluation and action staffs were members of different organizations, and awards where the evaluation and action staffs worked independently of one another.

Techniques Used to Analyze Data

In the introductory part of this chapter, we noted our concern for the level of sophistication of the type of data-analytic techniques used by evaluators in measuring process. We noted too that, while complex methods are not inherently better than less complex methods, usually one can assume that analyses would profit by the use of advanced techniques—e.g., multivariate analyses—if only to supplement qualitative findings. Since multivariate procedures allow the researcher to examine complex relationships among variables, their use is highly recommended. For example, take the case of an evaluation of the effect of a community mental-health center in dealing with disturbed children. It is almost certainly true that there will not be just one critical relationship between two variables, such as being in a therapy program and reducing the amount of antisocial behavior. Rather, there will be multiple relationships that enter into any attempt to explain if the therapy program is effective. Variables such as the family background of the child, social class of the therapist, and the like, may interact with the treatment and be important in any model of participation in the treatment. Thus, it is necessary to utilize techniques which will allow the evaluator to simultaneously examine multiple relationships in understanding process, that is, program implementation. Indeed, most evaluations are assessments of programs with multiple goals aimed at multiple groups, and it seems reasonable to conclude that in general all evaluations would do well to include, at least as part of their analytical procedures, some multivariate analyses.

Accordingly, when we ordered the responses to our question ascertaining the types of procedures used, we did it in such a way that the most advanced procedure was used to decide how we categorized the study. For example, an evaluation including narrative data, ratings from qualitative data, and multivariate statistical procedures was coded as "multivariate." Similarly, an evaluation using ratings from qualitative data and simple descriptive techniques was coded as "simple descriptive." The distribution then on the variable "type of data-analytic techniques used" is as follows.

For *only* those evaluations that included procedures to measure process ($N = 185$), 52 percent made use, at least in part, of multivariate statistical procedures; 37 percent used simple descriptive statistics; 6 percent assigned ratings to their qualitative data; and 5 percent relied only on the analysis of narrative or impressionistic summaries. In effect, then, given our assertion that evaluations should include some multivariate analyses, 48 percent of those who did assess process fell short of what can be considered a requirement of sound research. And if you add this group to those who never included measures to assess process at all, then only 41 percent can be said to have met the basic requirements for conducting adequate research.

While the argument can sometimes be made, we know it is not always the inappropriateness of multivariate statistics that results in the non-use of multivariate techniques about one-half of the time. For example, take the case of the evaluation study testing the effectiveness of a program to train unskilled workers to do residential rehabilitation. The analysis of the data was limited to the examination of narrative descriptive reports, impressionistic summaries, and some simple descriptive statistical procedures. The data were collected in narrative form as case histories and these narrative case histories were supplemented by the evaluator's review of the action-program records and reports. It would seem that, given the size of the sample that the evaluator was using, a budget of over $400,000, and a three-year time period, the evaluation could have been more sophisticated statistically. For instance, rather than testing a complex model which might have explained some variation in program implementation and success, this evaluation was based on a naive theoretical formulation which asserted that there should be an expected positive effect—i.e., unskilled workers should be able to rehabilitate homes, since "anyone can be trained to do rehabilitation of homes." Rather than citing other cases of evaluations that seemingly could have made use of more advanced data-analytic techniques, we wish to see if we can pinpoint some of the characteristics of those evaluations where multivariate techniques were employed (Table 4.2).

The findings of Table 4.2 are much like those of Table 4.1. First, on the left-hand side of the table—those evaluations which used multivariate statistical techniques to analyze their data—we find that many of the characteristics of what has been called the academic-type evaluation are over-represented. Studies in this group were largely grants, funded by the research-oriented agencies, of longer duration, undertaken largely by evaluators in nonprofit organizations (primarily universities), by persons holding doctoral degrees, and by evaluators defining their major audience as academic.

It is somewhat more difficult to interpret the right side of the table.

Table 4.2. Summary Table of Variables Associated (p<.05) with the Uses of Multivariate Statistical Techniques

| Variable | (N = 185) Techniques | |
	(N = 97) Of Those Studies Which Used Multivariate Statistical Techniques to Analyze Their Data	(N = 88) Of Those Studies* Which Did Not Include Multivariate Statistical Techniques to Analyze Their Data
Nature of award	37% were contracts 63% were grants	51% were contracts 49% were grants
Sponsoring agency	36% OE, other HEW, HUD, Agriculture, Labor, or OEO 64% NIH, NIMH, SRS, Justice	46% OE, other HEW, HUD, Agriculture, Labor, or OEO 54% NIH, NIMH, SRS, Justice
Length of study	22% less than 18 months 78% 18 months or more	48% less than 18 months 52% more than 18 months
Type of organization	22% profit corporations 78% nonprofit corporations	35% profit corporations 65% nonprofit corporations
Degree of project director	34% degrees less than doctorates 66% doctorates	54% degrees less than doctorate 46% doctorates
Major audience to whom findings are addressed	40% defined their audience as academic 60% did not define their audience as academic	18% defined their audience as academic 82% did not define their audience as academic

* See Footnote, Table 4.1

As was the case in Table 4.1, the same characteristics that generally were underrepresented (relative to their proportion in the population of evaluations examined) among those who used the more adequate procedures, generally were overrepresented among those who used less adequate procedures. For example, recall that of the 185 evaluations which included procedures to measure process, 28 percent were done by evaluators in profit-making research corporations and 72 percent by evaluators in non-profit organizations. Profit-making corporations are somewhat underrepresented among research groups that use multivariate procedures. Only 22 percent rather than the expected 28 percent used what we consider the more appropriate analytical procedures.

In conclusion, we note that the characteristics associated with the academic-type study are those correlated with the use of multivariate statistical techniques, just as they are the correlates of the use of more rigorous sampling procedures. To see if the patterns continue, we shall examine the last variable in this section, the *nature of the analysis*—that is, whether it was quantitative, qualitative, or evenly divided between the two.

Nature of the Analysis

In evaluation research, as in other modes of social research, there is a long-term debate between advocates of quantitative- and qualitative-type analyses. In the end, as has been noted by many, the research problem should determine the method. But for evaluation studies we believe that quantification is generally demanded. In no way is this meant to demean the value of qualitative research, but rather only to assert that given evaluation-research priorities and problems, quantitative methods seem better able to meet the demands.

First, of those evaluations which included procedures to measure process, what percentage used quantitative techniques to do so? We found that 44 percent categorized their evaluations as solely quantitative, 37 percent indicated that their evaluations were both quantitative and qualitative, and the remaining 18 percent categorized their efforts as qualitative. We were surprised that 18 percent were qualitative, in view of the strong advocacy of both policy personnel and persons who write about evaluation research toward quantitative investigations (Freeman and Sherwood 1965; Suchman 1967; Fairweather 1967; Hyman and Wright 1967; and Bernstein and Sheldon 1975).

Next, which studies use quantitative methods, and are the characteristics of those studies similar to those correlated with the use of adequate sampling procedures and sophisticated types of data-analytic techniques? In Table 4.3, we show the characteristics of studies associated with using

Table 4.3. Summary Table of Variables Statistically Associated (p<.05) with Analytic Approach

	Analytical Approach		
Variables	(N = 82) Of Those Evaluations Which Used Primarily Quantitative Methods	(N = 69) Of Those Evaluations Which Used Primarily Quantitative and Qualitative Methods	(N = 34)* Of those Evaluations Which Used Primarily Qualitative Methods
Nature of award	70% were grants 30% were contracts	46% were grants 54% were contracts	43% were grants 57% were contracts
Sponsoring agency	30% OE, other HEW, HUD, Agriculture, Labor, and OEO 70% NIH, NIMH, SRS, or Justice	48% OE, other HEW, HUD, Agriculture, Labor, or OEO 52% NIH, NIMH, or Justice	50% OE, other HEW, HUD, Agriculture, Labor, or OEO 50% NIH, NIMH, SRS, or Justice
Length of study	22% less than 18 months 78% more than 18 months	38% less than 18 months 62% more than 18 months	56% less than 18 months 44% more than 18 months
Type of organization	15% profit 85% nonprofit	41% profit 59% nonprofit	35% profit 65% nonprofit
Project director's degree	29% not doctorates 71% doctorates	57% not doctorates 43% doctorates	53% not doctorates 47% doctorates
Major audience to whom findings are addressed	40% academic 60% nonacademic	22% academic 78% nonacademic	21% academic 79% nonacademic

* See Footnote, Table 4.1.

quantitative methods only, those using qualitative methods only, or some combination of the two. We opt here *not* to reduce the dependent variable "nature of data analysis" to a dichotomy because of the differences between the three groups.

As shown in Table 4.3, the same characteristics found as correlates of the use of random sampling and multivariate statistical techniques are the characteristics correlated with the use of the recommended quantitative methods. That is, evaluations in which quantitative methods were the predominant mode of analysis tended to be grants; evaluations funded by NIH, NIMH, SRS, or Justice; studies of longer duration; studies done by evaluators in nonprofit organizations (largely universities); studies by evaluators with doctoral degrees; and studies by those defining their major audience as academic. Thus the pattern noted earlier is repeated a third time.

There is, however, one further important correlate in this instance, the academic discipline of the project director. Since, as shown later, this turns out to be a particularly important variable, Table 4.4 shows the relation-

Table 4.4. Project Director's Discipline and Data-Analytic Procedures Used

Nature of Data-Analytic Process	Academic Discipline					
	$(N=38)$ Eco-nomics	$(N=57)$ Psy-chology	$(N=28)$ Soci-ology	$(N=25)$ Educa-tion	$(N=30)$ Medicine, Psychiatry, Social Work	$(N=55)*$ Other†
Quantitative	29%	58%	43%	32%	20%	22%
Quantitative and qualitative	37	18	21	44	30	33
Qualitative	16	3	21	4	27	20
Evaluation didn't include procedures to measure process	18	21	14	20	23	26

$\chi^2 = 32.26$, p $<.01$
* Three cases omitted because of lack of information.
† Other includes public affairs, business administration, accounting, English, anthropology, etc.

ship between academic discipline and the nature of the data analysis used. Psychologists most frequently make use of quantitative methods. Before trying to explain this finding, however, we must recall that the psychologists in our sample were predominantly Ph.D.'s working in university settings. This was not, however, the case for others; for example, economists in our sample predominantly had no doctoral degrees and typically were not located in universities. Because this point will be important later, Table 4.5 provides the relationship between discipline and degree, and Table 4.6 gives the relationship between discipline, type of organization, and degree.

The major inference to be drawn from these tables is that it is unlikely that psychologists in general are better trained than, for example, econo-

Table 4.5. Project Director's Discipline and Highest Degree

	Discipline					
	$(N=38)$	$(N=57)$	$(N=28)$	$(N=25)$	$(N=30)$	$(N=55)*$
Highest Degree	Eco-nomics	Psy-chology	Soci-ology	Educa-tion	Medicine, Psychiatry, Social Work	Other
Ph.D.	39%	81%	57%	32%	3%	27%
Other doctorate (M.D., E.D.P., D.S.W.)	5	—	—	28	60	4
Master's	34	14	43	32	33	44
Bachelor's	21	5	—	8	3	26

$\chi^2 = 132.84$, p $<.001$
* Three cases omitted because of lack of information.

Table 4.6. Project Director's Discipline, Highest Degree, and Type of Organizational Affiliation

	Type of Organization			
	$(N = 64)$ Profit		$(N = 172)$ Nonprofit*	
	Degree of Project Director			
Academic Discipline	$(N = 40)$ B.A./M.A.	$(N = 22)$ Doctorate	$(N = 62)$ B.A./M.A.	$(N = 109)$ Doctorate
Economics	30%	27%	14%	10%
Psychology	5	9	14	40
Sociology	13	18	10	12
Education	10	14	10	11
Medicine, psychiatry, social work	—	5	18	17
Other	43	27	34	10

* Nonprofit here includes nonprofit research corporations, educational institutions, and public-service or planning agencies.

mists or more likely to use more appropriate methods of research. But the evaluators trained in economics in the study are not usually Ph.D. economists of the type generally found in universities; rather they are persons without doctoral degrees working in profit-making research corporations. The psychologists, however, much more often hold doctoral degrees and are working in university settings. In part, then, the findings here help to explain the differences noted in Table 4.4 regarding the way in which various disciplines fare on a measure indicative of methodological adequacy.

Before concluding with some summary remarks, we shall leave the statistical data to examine some case examples drawn from the studies we reviewed. We do so not to single out especially poor studies but rather to provide some concrete examples of what is revealed in the tables.

SOME EXAMPLES

We noted in our discussion of the various sampling procedures that a sizable proportion of evaluators used what we categorized as less than adequate techniques. For illustration, we cite the case of an evaluation which purported to test the effectiveness of a semiautomated single fingerprint system, a program aimed at increasing the number of crimes solved, as an example of the use of less than adequate methodological techniques. Rather than selecting a sample area of the city and a sample period of time in which to make observations in some random systematic fashion, the evaluator arbitrarily selected a part of the city and a time interval on the basis of convenience and easy availability. He did so despite the fact that there was no indication that either the area or the time period selected were representative of the city or the processing of fingerprints. Having no idea of how typical or atypical his sample was, he can not generalize to the population he was interested in, i.e., the entire city, with any degree of certainty. Thus, by failing to appropriately select a sample, he built into his evaluation severe limitations on the interpretation and use of any results he might find.

Similarly, in another evaluation, this one purporting to test the impact of "legal-service programs," data were also collected on arbitrarily selected legal-service bureaus. Federal policy-makers are interested not in any atypical programs which are either effective or ineffective in accomplishing their goals, but rather in the findings about those which *are* typical or representative of others being conducted so that general decisions about whether to terminate, modify, or expand legal-service programs can be based on information pertinent to all or most legal-service programs. Knowing that a particular program is being carried out as specified and that as such it is effective or ineffective, may be useful for that program. But what is most important is the evaluation of process in a group of programs which supposedly are representative of the range of extant programs; the way to increase the likelihood of having knowledge which can be generalized is to select a sample of programs in a fashion that provides representativeness. Interestingly, in both of these cases, as well as many others, there seemed to be no obvious reason for not having employed better sampling techniques.

Another important group of evaluations singled out in our analysis are those which used qualitative rather than quantitative methods or some combination of both. We have already discussed the case of an evaluation purporting to test the effectiveness of a training program for unskilled workers engaged in residential and neighborhood rehabilitation. Another, albeit less bizarre, example of what appears to be an inappropriate choice of methodological procedures was the case of the evaluation assessing the effect of a suicide-prevention center. The intent of that evaluation was to demonstrate (1) that the program had successfully been implemented according to stated guidelines and (2) that some change had occurred as a result of the implementation of the program. Implementation was evaluated solely on the basis of narrative accounts of the involvement of persons with the center. It is hard to understand, given the purposes of that evaluation, why the evaluator opted to rely solely on qualitative methods. It would seem, given the importance of the program, that he would have wanted to use the most convincing evidence available. At the very least, a mixture of quantitative and qualitative methods would have been more appropriate.

The following two studies are cited in order to give further credence to the position that, in general, evaluations which use the recommended or more appropriate methodologies on one dimension, such as sampling, also use the more appropriate methodology on other dimensions, e.g., multivariate analyses. That is, we are positing that these individual dimensions of sampling, statistical techniques, and nature of data analysis are correlated with one another and that taken together they can be said to represent relative quality or levels of methodological adequacy. Thus we contrast a study which is characteristic of the academic type with one representative of the entrepreneurial type.

The academic-type evaluation was a study aimed at assessing the impact of twenty-one neighborhood health centers, in an effort to determine how the health center improved conditions of community health. The evaluator collected data from participant observation, conducted structured interviews with the service personnel and target population, and reviewed the reports and records of the action agency to measure process. Further, the population on which he collected data was selected through the use of an area-probability sample. His method of data analysis included the use of ratings from qualitative data and descriptive and multivariate statistical procedures. When asked to characterize the nature of his analysis he indicated it was "quantitative." Within the limits of our study, it appears then that this evaluator was consistently following the recommended procedures meeting the fundamental requirements in carrying out good research.

A study with the characteristics of the entrepreneurial-type evaluation opted to use "softer" methods in its evaluation, which sought to assess the level of community participation in community mental-health centers. Here the project director indicated that the sample of persons to be interviewed included "groups, organizations, and individuals familiar with or involved in the program." Our contention is that a much more appropriate study group would have been a representative sample drawn from the area such that one could rule out the biases posed by the selection factor. The data-analysis techniques included reviews of narrative descriptive reports, impressionistic summaries, and a "tested questionnaire," but no quantitative analyses of it. Again our contention is that a more rigorous systematic and standardized analysis would have been more effective especially when one is working with such a biased sample. Needless to say, the evaluator described her study as being qualitative. We cannot avoid noting that this same study indicated, in response to the set of questions on methodological procedures used to assess impact, that no measures of outcome were taken at all. Barring some very unusual circumstances, we would conclude that this study is illustrative of an evaluation which did not meet the basic requirements necessary to be classified as competent evaluation research.

CONCLUSION

On the basis of the data presented thus far, it appears that of the 185 evaluations which included procedures to measure process, those that used what we regard as the most appropriate procedures were usually characterized by the following properties: the evaluation was likely to be (1) a grant, (2) sponsored by NIH-type agencies, (3) a study of more than eighteen months, (4) one where the evaluator was affiliated with a non-profit organization, usually a university, (5) one where the project director held a doctorate, most often a Ph.D., (6) one where the project director received his or her advanced training in psychology, (7) one where the evaluator defined other colleagues and researchers as the major audience to whom findings would be addressed, and (8) one where the evaluation and action staffs worked *interdependently* but as separate units within the same organization that undertook the action program.

Not all of the characteristics discussed in Chapter 3 as delineating the academic and entrepreneurial types of research endeavors consistently appear as statistically significant correlates of the three measures of quality that were introduced to assess process. In general, however, the polar types have utility in explaining the conduct of process evaluations.

Table 6.4. Quality of the Research by Nature of the Award, Sponsoring Agency, and Length of Study

	Grant				Contract			
	Research Agency*		Operating Agency		Research Agency		Operating Agency	
Index of Research Quality	(N = 51) More than 2 years	(N = 30) Less than 2 years	(N = 6) More than 2 years	(N = 1) Less than 2 years	(N = 5) More than 2 years	(N = 6) Less than 2 years	(N = 14) More than 2 years	(N = 37)† Less than 2 years
High (5.6–6.0)	20%	23%	50%	100%	—	—	14%	5%
Medium (4.2–5.6)	47	27	17	—	40%	67%	29	19
Low (0–4.1)	33	50	33	—	60	83	57	76

* Research agencies include NIH, NIMH, SRS, and Justice. Operating agencies include OE, OEO, Agriculture, Labor, HUD, and HEW *other than* SRS, NIH, and NIMH.
† No information on 2 studies.

The general tone of the explanation is prefaced best by a statement from Polanyi (1951, p. 90).

> The pursuit of science can be organized therefore, in no other manner than by granting complete independence to all mature scientists. . . . The function of public authorities is not to plan research, but only to provide opportunities for its pursuit. . . . To do less is to neglect the progress of science; to do more is to cultivate mediocrity and waste public money.

The consequences of an award being a grant or contract seem to be related to four dimensions. The first has to do with what may be termed "the glory of pure research." While one may argue about the current appropriateness of this ideological stance, it is still a most common tenet among academic scientists. Implicit in much of the socialization process that scientists experience is an assertion that the invocation of utilitarian concerns reduces the quality of one's work by obstructing true scientific pursuit. By imposing issues which are external to the processes that yield the discovery of knowledge, the purity of the endeavor is thwarted.

Weber (1946) posited that academic men "engage in science for science' sake" and not merely because others want or need their results. Merton (1949), taking a stronger stance, posited that one of the basic tenets of science is *not* to be anyone's handmaiden. Further, he contended, science is often weakened when it is judged by utilitarian criteria. Parsons (1951) noted that there is a high value placed on understanding the empirical world apart from the applicability of the results of that understanding. And finally, Hagstrom (1965), in his study of the scientific community, reminded us that work for practical purposes is not only less prestigious in the eyes of the academic community, but that some go so far as to label "deviant" the pursuit of research problems which are of applied significance *only*.

The second dimension has to do with the specificity of the research focus, and the autonomy of the researcher. The literature consistently suggests that (1) scientists are motivated best when they operate autonomously and (2) productivity is higher when the degrees of research freedom are greater. It has been asserted that one of the basic norms of science is the autonomy of the scientist and thus external controls are threatening to the endeavor. Roe (1952) in a study of eminent scientists noted that the single most important factor in the development of a scientist was the freedom to follow one's own interests without direction or interference. Similarly, Shils (1956), Whyte (1956), and Kornhauser (1962) found that intellectual curiosity, which stimulates good work, is dampened by an overly structured problem. Marcson (1966) in a study of scientists in government delineates "autonomy" as one incentive which motivates scientists to do good work, along with recognition and self-realization. Thus, we conclude that a priori specification of the research problem probably hampers the autonomy of the researcher and as such is less likely to motivate high-quality work.

The third dimension, closely related to the above, deals with the voluntary selection of a problem. Both Kornhauser (1962) and Hagstrom (1965) underscore the importance of the selection of the problem being initiated by the scientist. The rationale given is that freedom to pursue one's own interests is a primary incentive for doing good work and thus enables one to maximize his or her contribution to science.

The fourth dimension, somewhat unrelated to the others, has to do with a more practical consequence of the way in which contracts differ from grants. Grants are more likely to be subjected to peer review and as such those funded represent studies which have been carefully screened and approved by a committee of experts. In 1964 a committee on Science and Public Policy recommended that all research awards be prescreened by study sections or advisory panels, but to date only some of the grant-giving divisions of the various parts of NIH/NIMH and NSF seem to have uniformly adopted this recommendation. Additionally, because of the way in which contracts are ordinarily awarded, the number of competitors is limited to those researchers who can make themselves easily available for a new task. Grant requests, on the other hand, are accepted continuously but reviewed at specified time intervals, and there is normally a constant flow of applicants for the scarce resources. It is this lesser amount of competition which the literature points to as being a negative characteristic; Ben-David (1960) and numerous others in their respective studies of scientists suggest that parochialism and deviation from scientific goals are more likely to occur when the competition for rewards is less.

We conclude that while there is nothing inherently superior in grants, in comparing the nature of grants to contracts, the former are far more academically oriented and therefore probably better suited to the "scientific" tradition than contracts. As such we can further assume that on the whole those who work on grants are working under conditions more conducive to higher quality research than those who work on contracts.

The second variable, "sponsoring agency," is equally interesting but more difficult to explain as a correlate of quality. Two points, however, can be put forth. One is that NIH/NIMH, the agencies where peer review is most prevalent, fund studies which often are judged to be in the highest research-quality category. However, this is only true for their grants, where the peer-review system was operating, not for their contracts. (Peer review has since been extended to some of their contract research but this was not common at the time of our study.) Second, where there is relatively little peer review, i.e., in SRS or LEAA, there seems to be less difference in the quality of the grants as compared to contracts, although because the number of contracts is so small, no definitive conclusions can be drawn. What this may suggest is that it is the way in which research is funded— i.e., the standards applied, the reviewers, the amount of competition, and so on—which makes the difference. Further, as suggested, section heads and research "managers" in NIH and NIMH are most likely to be drawn from academic environments, and as such their funding of higher quality research might reflect their greater ability to judge methodological rigor and expertise as demonstrated in submitted proposals, as compared to ad-ministrators of other agencies who have less formal methodological and substantive training.

Length of study, the other variable of importance, is one which requires that certain assumptions be made in order to cast its differing categories into our explanatory framework. The first assumption is that, as Parsons (1951), Kornhauser (1962), and Hagstrom (1965) all have noted, scien-tists are trained to be cautious in their work, and to be careful about draw-ing conclusions and positing assertions. That is, part of the socialization of becoming a scientist involves the recognition of the importance of deep, *lengthy* probes and the exhaustive testing and retesting of ideas. Character-istically, the scientist believes that his or her results have implications both for one's professional career and for society at large and as such, one cannot afford to rush to answers. In fact, hasty publication or release of findings before the completion of the analysis is viewed as a form of scien-tific deviation.

Kornhauser (1962) makes a further point asserting that the more the emphasis is on long-term research, the stronger the pressure is to or-ganize the work on a professional basis. The implication is that short-term projects lead to task groups which are more "project" than "professionally" oriented. Since project-oriented groups tend to produce lower-quality re-search, this is a consequence with which one must deal. Finally, we note that since the majority of scientists are located in universities, the writing of research proposals are tasks they wish to undertake as infrequently as pos-sible since they are means, not ends, in themselves. It is likely that the more academically-oriented researchers choose to work on studies of longer dura-tion since they are more congruent with their work environment and needs.

In line with the framework we are using, we can conclude that the longer studies were probably more appropriately characterized as being reflective of an "academic-scientific orientation" than the studies of shorter duration. And again, our data indicate that the more academiclike charac-teristic, i.e., longer studies, is related to higher research quality.

In summary, it appears that if one were to order each of the possible conditions along a continuum, where one end was most congruent with traditional scientific norms and the other least congruent, or what we have described as academic versus entrepreneurial, those most congruent would be evaluations funded as grants, for longer periods of time, and funded as a result of a highly competitive process wherein awards were made on the basis of the demonstrated methodological and theoretical expertise of the evaluator as judged by a panel of experts. Given that past research tells us that the more "scientific" one's orientation—i.e., the more one subscribes to scientific norms—the greater the likelihood that one's research will be of high quality, it becomes possible to understand why grants funded by NIH and NIMH for longer periods of time would fare highest on our index of research quality. Additionally, the practical facts that contract proposals are formulated more hurriedly, and that they are carried out in shorter time spans, often on poorly defined programs, make our findings all the more understandable. Moreover, when we later discuss the types of organization in relation to research quality, we will gain further insight into the differences just noted.

Characteristics of the Evaluation Study

This domain deals essentially with two ideas: the complexity of the evaluation and action program, and the theoretical framework in which it is grounded. With respect to the first notion, it has often been said that some research is executed with greater facility than other research because of the nature and the complexity of the problem being addressed. It has been asserted, for example, that evaluation studies attempting to assess extremely complex programs, such as the negative income tax experiment, become extremely complicated themselves, and turn out to be methodologically less adequate than studies of simpler action programs.

The second element focuses on the theoretical framework. Hagstrom (1965), Wholey et al. (1970), and Stromsdorfer (1972) point to the fact that higher quality research is correlated with the conducting of one's research within some formal theoretical framework, regardless of the framework used. Accordingly, we suppose that it does not matter whether one uses an economic, a social-psychological model, or any other theoretical framework, but only that there be one. As reported in Chapter 3, surprisingly few evaluations were conducted on action programs guided by a formal theoretical framework.

Turning first to an examination of the amount of variance explained by this set of dimensions, characteristics of the evaluation study, we find that while it does not seem to be as large a determinant as the first domain —characteristics of the award—the R^2 is equal to .14, significant at the .01 level. However, controlling for other domains (characteristics of the award, of the research unit, and the interorganizational network), *this domain only explains 1 percent of the variation*. This indicates that in and of itself this set of characteristics does not have much explanatory power. By examining the contribution of each of the component variables, perhaps we can discern which seem to be important correlates of high-quality research and which are not. Tables 6.5 and 6.6 provide us with that information.

As can be seen in Table 6.5, neither the number of targets studied— e.g., whether they studied the recipients of the action program or the recipients and the staff—nor the complexity of the study—e.g., whether it was a national multifocused controversial program or not—seemed to matter in terms of variation in measured research quality. The substantive focus did seem to be significant, and the nature of the theoretical framework was most important.

Table 6.5. Amount of Variance Explained by Characteristics of the Study

	Number of Targets Studied	Complexity of Study	Focus of Action Program	Theoretical Framework
Amount of variance explained	0	0	6%*	12%†

* $= p < .05$
† $= p < .001$

Table 6.6 shows that evaluators studying health and mental-health programs fared better than their counterparts in quality. However, the foci of studies are highly correlated with the sponsoring agencies, e.g., NIH and NIMH fund evaluations of health programs. Because the sponsoring agency is a stronger correlate of quality, we shall not concern ourselves with "focus" as an important variable since it is most probably a surrogate for the sponsoring agency.

With respect to the nature of the theoretical framework, those evaluations guided by a formal theoretical model did much better on our index than those guided by a social-service model or those guided by no model at all.

As reported in Chapter 3, complexity, focus, and nature of theoretical framework seem unrelated to one another in any systematic fashion. Given this, coupled with what we have just gleaned from the data, we conclude that the major variable of importance here is the nature of the theoretical framework, or rather the presence or absence of such a framework. When there is no theory guiding the research, there is a greater likelihood of low-

Table 6.6. Research Quality and Characteristics of the Study

	Deviation from Overall Mean
Number of Targets	
None	+.1
One of three	—.1
All three	—.1
Complexity of the Program Evaluation	
Less complex	—
Especially complex	—.2
Focus of the Action Program Evaluated	
Health or mental health	+.3
Public safety	+.2
Education	+.1
Income security, housing, welfare	—.5
Nature of Theoretical Framework	
Formal theory, e.g., economics, social structural, social psychological	+.9
Medical or social-service model	—.2
No theory	—.4

quality research, whereas when there is a formal theoretical framework, there is a greater likelihood that the research will be more methodologically adequate (Table 6.7).

Why is the presence of a formal theory correlated with higher quality research? Following the same line of argument developed earlier, we note that past efforts to study the correlates of higher quality research have suggested that the more one is committed to the tenets of science, the greater the likelihood that one's research will make a theoretical contribution. Insofar as one of the primary goals of scientists is to display their methodological competence through handling theoretically important problems, it is unlikely that persons committed to scientific excellence would conduct

Table 6.7. Quality of Comprehensive Evaluations and Framework of Study

Research Quality	Nature of Theoretical Framework		
	$(N = 34)$ Formal Theory	$(N = 103)$ Service Model	$(N = 15)$ No Theory
High	37%	10%	27%
Medium	36	31	27
Low	27	59	47

$\chi^2 = 16.60$, p $< .01$

their research without some formal theoretical model to guide their efforts. This is especially so since the scientific community, according to Hagstrom (1965) confers the highest prestige upon works which make the greatest theoretical contributions. In our polar classification, we regard concern with a theoretical framework as characteristic of the academic-research type.

Since evaluation research generally is stimulated by utilitarian concerns, without consideration for its theoretical relevance, it is often up to the evaluator to ground his or her research efforts into some formal framework according to how he or she defines the problem. That this, however, should not be a haphazard enterprise is obvious. The advantage of having a theoretical framework is that it provides a body of past research which can be examined, and as such it facilitates the deduction of hypotheses, points out what can be expected to be key variables, and the like. Evaluation research has theoretical potential in terms of understanding social change, but it is the task of the evaluator to make that research theoretically relevant. In so doing, one conforms to a dictum of the scientific community; in not doing this, one decreases the quality of his or her research.

Characteristics of the Evaluation-Research Unit

Much has been written by those who have studied scientific productivity about the relationship between the researcher (e.g., his or her academic degree, years of experience, and so on) and the quality of the research (e.g., Barnes 1971). There have also been many studies on the organizations with which researchers are affiliated in relation to research quality. Concerning the scientist, and in this case the evaluator, the expectation would be that the more advanced the training, the more likely one is to produce excellent work. Insofar as advanced graduate education includes not only learning specific methodological techniques but also a general appreciation of the "scientific method," one would expect persons with the most advanced degrees to use the most appropriate research procedures.

With respect to the organizational affiliation, it is suggested that the context in which one works largely determines the reward structure, the lines of authority, the degree of autonomy, the locus of responsibility for work, and the major audience to which findings will be addressed (Hagstrom 1965). It is held that these factors are strongly correlated with research quality. That is, higher-quality research is associated with (1) having a reward system that counts heavily on published works demonstrating theoretical and methodological excellence (Blume and Sinclair 1972), (2) basing an authority structure on colleague rather than hierarchical control (Kornhauser 1962), (3) affording the scientists the greatest degree of freedom in determining which problems to research and how to carry out that research (Whyte 1956; Kornhauser 1962; Hagstrom 1965), (4) holding the scientist directly responsible for his or her work, and (5) defining the major audience as other professionals and interested researchers. The organization, then, which maximizes these conditions is said to be most conducive to the production of higher quality research.

Repeatedly and consistently, it is argued that the university setting provides the work milieu most congruent with the conditions under which high-quality research flourishes (Ben-David 1960; Gordon and Marquis 1966; Rossi and Williams 1972). Further, it is probable that the more the organizational setting differs from the universitylike establishment, the more likely there will be deviation from scientific norms and adherence to some other set of norms. Implicitly, this means that insofar as profit-making research corporations operate within a different normative framework, for example, by rewarding individuals for merely getting grants and contracts, they are less likely to be concerned about scientific excellence.

Our data, as expected, show that taken together the variables—(1) the number of awards to the organization, (2) the geographic location of the organization, (3) the type of organization, (4) the relative prestige of the organization, (5) the highest degree of the project director, (6) the years of related experience of the project director, (7) the academic discipline of the project director, and (8) the major audience to which findings are addressed—explain 32 percent of the variance ($p < .001$) in research quality among comprehensive evaluations. Moreover, controlling for the contribution of the other sets of characteristics, this set still explains 7 percent of the variance.

Given that this set of characteristics is an important correlate of research quality, the next point of interest is to determine which of the individual variables are most important. Whether an organization has multiple awards or not seems to make little significant difference in terms of research quality. The prestige of the organization, the geographic region in which it is located, the project director's years of experience, and the highest earned degree of the project director also seem to be of minor importance (Table 6.8). Perhaps the most surprising of these is that the academic degree did not turn out to be a statistically significant correlate, although those with Ph.D. degrees did fare best when looked at separately. This implies that the degree is not as important as the organization with which one is affiliated; it is the organization that largely sets the pace. In our sample, most of the persons with Ph.D. degrees were affiliated with universities or university-research centers, and universities ranked high above the other organizations in terms of their score on our index. Table 6.9 will clarify this important relationship. Note that while there is a statistically significant

Table 6.8. Amount of Variance Explained by Characteristics of Research Unit

	Amount of Variance Explained
Academic discipline of project director	14%*
Major audience to whom findings were addressed	8†
Type of organization conducting evaluation	7‡
Highest degree of project director	3
Geographic location of organization	3
Multiple awards to organization	2
Experience of project director	1
Prestige of organization	0

$* = p < .001$
$† = p < .01$
$‡ = p < .05$

relationship between research quality and degree, when the type of organization is controlled, the relationship is no longer significant.

The variables which are most important in terms of their statistically significant relationship to the quality of the research include (1) the academic discipline of the project director, (2) the major audience to which findings are addressed, and (3) the type of organization conducting the evaluation.

From Table 6.10 we infer that higher quality research in evaluation studies is correlated with (1) having the evaluation conducted by a project director whose academic discipline is psychology, (2) having the research conducted by a staff affiliated with or working in a university setting, and (3) having the evaluator define the major audience as other professionals and colleagues. Because the academic discipline of the project director is such an important variable, Table 6.11 shows its relationship to research quality.

By way of summary information, Table 6.12 presents the characteristics of evaluations scoring high versus those which score medium or low on our index of comprehensive research quality. There are more marked differences in the "high group," suggesting that variables identified as correlates of quality are necessary but not sufficient; the likelihood of greater quality is increased when these conditions are present, but their presence is not a guarantee of higher quality. As before, the set of conditions which are correlated with higher quality evaluation research is the set labeled in earlier chapters as academic-type evaluations. Since later we will show a more exact estimate of predicted quality, we shall now try to understand why the characteristics of the research unit have such an important effect on quality.

Table 6.9. Project Director's Highest Degree and the Quality of the Research, Controlling for the Type of Organization

	Type of Organization							
	Profit or Service Organization				University or Nonprofit Organization			
	Degree							
Research Quality	(N = 12) B.A.	(N = 30) M.A.	(N = 6) Other Dr.	(N = 24) Ph.D.	(N = 4) B.A.	(N = 21) M.A.	(N = 16) Other Dr.	(N = 39) Ph.D.
High	8%	3%	17%	17%	—	14%	19%	2%
Medium	42	27	33	33	50%	38	13	33
Low	50	70	50	50	50	48	68	33

$\chi^2 = 4.61$, p is not significant.
$\chi^2 = 9.28$, p is not significant.

Table 6.10. Characteristics of Research Unit and Quality

	Deviation from Overall Mean
Academic Discipline of Project Director	
Psychology	+.9
Education	−.2
Other	−.2
Medicine, psychiatry, social work	−.3
Economics	−.4
Sociology	−.5
Major Audience	
Academic	+.6
Nonacademic	−.3
Type of Organization	
Educational institution	+.5
Nonprofit research corporation	—
Public-service or planning agency	−.1
Profit-making research corporation	−.5

Table 6.11. Project Director's Academic Discipline and Research Quality

	Discipline					
	$(N = 24)$	$(N = 38)$	$(N = 19)$	$(N = 19)$	$(N = 21)$ Medicine, Psychiatry,	$(N = 31)$
Quality	Economics	Psychology	Sociology	Education	Social Work	Other
High	4%	32%	16%	26%	5%	12%
Medium	38	47	5	21	33	29
Low	58	21	79	53	62	58

$\chi^2 = 28.92$, p $<.01$

One could now ask why certain variables, like the type of organization, seem to be so strongly correlated with research quality. We know from past efforts that the organizational context plays a key role in shaping the work. However, the fact that university settings seem more conducive to the production of more adequate evaluations necessitates some discussion.

We begin with a discussion of the type of organization, since it requires a rather lengthy presentation much like the "nature of the award" discussed earlier. We have already asserted that the organization in which one works influences the behavior which results. Using Kornhauser's (1962) specification of four areas of organizational conflict and accommodation, plus one we shall add, allows us to present the material more coherently.

Table 6.12. Characteristics of Comprehensive Evaluation Studies Scoring High, Medium, or Low on Research Quality

	Quality		
	(N = 27) Of those who score High	(N = 49) Of those who score Medium	(N = 76)* Of those who score Low
Type of organization:	27% were profit/service 73% were university/ nonprofit	48% were profit/service 52% were university/ nonprofit	54% were profit/service 46% were university/ nonprofit
Major audience to whom findings are addressed:	46% academic 54% nonacademic	35% academic 65% nonacademic	20% academic 80% nonacademic
Highest earned degree of project director:	19% nondoctorate 81% doctorate	48% nondoctorate 52% doctorate	50% nondoctorate 50% doctorate

* See Table 6.1.

We shall proceed by dividing our discussion into organizational (1) assets, (2) goals, (3) incentives, (4) control, and (5) responsibility.

With respect to some general assets, the university is posited to be the organization where most scientists are found, and the organization wherein the most prestigious scholars have been noted to reside (Bello 1956). It is purported to be viewed by the scientific community as highest in status (Hagstrom 1965), and the institution which can be said most to protect, sustain, and embody the norms with which the scientist most closely identifies (Parsons 1951).

Generally, the university integrates the scientist into its community because of shared values, and in so doing reinforces the commitment to scientific norms. Shepard (1954), Merton (1957), Caplow and McGee (1958), and others in their respective works delineate the goals set forth by the university for its members to be (1) the pursuit of knowledge and ideas for the sake of knowledge, the enhancement of science, and the betterment of society; (2) the publication of research findings which demonstrate methodological expertise, theoretical relevance, and originality of thought; and (3) the participation in activities, research or otherwise, recognized by the scientific community to be relevant to the development of one's professional career. Hagstrom (1965) suggests that the scientist conforms because conformity gains him or her the rewards of the institution, e.g., promotion, and the acceptance and confirmation of status by his or her colleagues in the larger scientific community. The rules for this exchange system and the appreciation of the meaning of the sanctions are learned as part of socialization into the scientific profession.

Closely related to the goals are the incentives which operate as motivating factors. In addition to those noted generally above, the desire for recognition by one's colleagues must be singled out as a primary motive for doing "high-quality work." Since one is evaluated both in the university and the scientific community on the basis of scholarly contributions, it becomes most important to conduct research in methodologically sound ways so that the findings will be acceptable to others.

The notion of control as being important is brought out by Kornhauser (1962) in his study comparing universities to industrial organizations as research settings. One major thrust of his argument is that universities are characterized by colleague control whereas industry is characterized by hierarchical control. The implication is that colleague control is based on the application of a set of standards derived from the norms of the scientific community. Under hierarchical control, nonscientists may rule the organization and institute a normative structure where nonscientific contributions are rewarded equally or more than scientific ones. It has been shown that this latter kind of arrangement often thwarts the production of sound research.

The locus of responsibility is important in that the more the scientist is personally accountable for his or her work, the less likely one is to deviate from scientific standards. In the university the presence of watchful colleagues and of students, whose task it is to critically examine, serves to "keep the scientist honest." Additionally, almost all university scientists publish under their name alone or in collaboration with one or two other carefully chosen scientists. For the scientists in nonuniversity settings, however, it is not uncommon to publish under the "company name," therefore diffusing the locus of responsibility.

In conclusion, the general assets of the university plus the assets provided by its particular structuring of goals, control, incentives, and assignment of responsibility, all help to support the premise that the university as an institution most closely embodies the values of science. It is thus not surprising that our data indicate that evaluators in university settings produce higher quality research than those in other types of organizations. There are, however, drawbacks which occur when evaluators are in university settings, which shall be discussed later.

Our data indicated that the lowest quality research is most often correlated with being located in the organizational setting of the profit-making corporation. The research staff in a profit-making organization tends to be unilateral because most prefer a relatively homogeneous staff. This results in a liability because such a structure does not incorporate a range of highly specialized persons whose expertise covers a broad spectrum and whose assistance in special areas might be useful. Moreover, since the organization is "group" rather than individually oriented, the check system of colleague control which helps force persons to justify their work is less operative. Additionally, there are problems posed by operating outside one's "natural" surroundings. That is, outside the university communication channels between colleagues are curtailed. Whyte (1956), for example, noted that few scientists in industry know one another or one another's work or are known to other colleagues.

One further liability is that in the purist, albeit unrealistic sense, "science has no clients." Scientists in profit-making organizations have two clients and this makes their position more difficult. In agreeing to conduct an evaluation, they take on the federal sponsoring agency as a client (as do university persons) but they also must simultaneously serve the organization in which they work.

The incentives which guide the researcher in a profit-making corporation are defined by the reward structure of that organization. It appears that rewards are based on securing contracts or grants and "doing the work" of the organization. Contributions to the scientific community, however, such as papers in refereed journals and at professional meetings usually are minimally recognized. Characteristically, then, the reward structure is "local" rather than "cosmopolitan." Gouldner (1957) finds a local orientation to be negatively correlated with high productivity.

The other two types of organizations, nonprofit research corporations and public-service/planning agencies are relatively easy to locate in this scheme. Nonprofit research corporations seem to model themselves most after the university research centers, but do not have the formal university ties. They share the university goal-reward structure, but do not share in all the assets, e.g., the presence of various specialists, the prestige, the colleagueship, and the like. As expected then, since the characteristics of their working environment are more congruent with scientific values, the quality of their research should be poorer than that of the university but better than those in profit corporations. Our data indicates this to be the case.

As for the public-service and planning agencies, we know little about how scientists operate in this setting. Marcson (1966) in his study of scientists in government, points out that the major problem is not so much a conflict of goals (as in the profit corporation) but multiple goals. While university persons have multiple goals, teaching and service (Caplow and McGee 1958; Boalt and Lantz 1970), there is agreement that the pursuit of science always comes first. Public-service and planning agencies by definition, however, must attend to the goals of providing services and public administration. And we know too that often the goal of service is antagonistic to scientific investigation. It is unclear where the priorities lie. Further, the incentives, rewards, control structure, and locus of responsibility are here more characteristically akin to those which typify corporations rather than universities, and as such they are likely to take their similar toll on the quality of the research.

If we posit, in accordance with past studies of quality in scientific research, that the stronger the scientific orientation, the higher the quality of the research, then one should expect the highest quality research to be found among evaluators in universities where the scientific orientation is likely to be strongest, followed by nonprofit research corporations, service agencies, and profit corporations, the latter being most unlike the former. Table 6.10 shows that our data support this expectation.

The next important variable in this set of characteristics of the research unit, major audience, is so closely related to the others that only brief mention of some few points need be made. Blau (1955), Gouldner (1957), Lazarsfeld and Thielens (1958), Kornhauser (1962), Hagstrom (1965), and others in their respective works all imply that the more one defines one's major audience as academic, i.e., the scientific community, the greater is the likelihood that the scientific norms will be strictly followed. This is explained by the fact that the nature of one's reference group defines one's goals as well as the means of goal attainment. The commitment to the goals of publication of sound research and communication with colleagues is believed reinforcing and helpful in preventing deviation from scientific norms. As Hagstrom (1965:43) has stated: "The set of persons with whom most communication is maintained will probably have the greatest influence on the scientist's own perspective." Our data support this thesis: when the evaluator defined the major audience as academic, the research product is most likely to be of high quality. Since publications in referred journals are likely to be subjected to extreme scrutiny, especially in terms of their methodological soundness, it is easy to understand why this variable turns out to be significant.

The one variable left to discuss is academic discipline. This is a particularly problematic area perhaps because one is hard pressed to explain why psychologists seem to so outdo the others in the quality of their research. Admittedly they represent the discipline most oriented toward experimentation, but that was only one of six factors on which "quality" was judged. It has been suggested too that psychology is the discipline that most intensively trains persons simultaneously to be service-oriented and science-oriented, and as such evaluation research is an area with which they would feel more comfortable. Further, psychology may be "more of a science" than sociology and economics, and certainly their research techniques are better developed. While granting tentatively that all of these claims contain an element of truth, our skepticism led us to examine the relationship of academic discipline to the other characteristics deemed as reflecting a scientific orientation. The correlation matrix is shown in Table 6.13.

Being a psychologist is highly correlated with all the other conditions associated with higher quality research, and being an economist is negatively correlated with those conditions. Thus, in addition perhaps to better training, psychologists are found most often in contextual settings that encourage quality work. Further, note that the pattern for those in medicine, social work, and psychiatry is much like the one for psychologists, *except* that their work is less likely to be of long duration and not likely to be guided by a formal theoretical framework. That probably explains why on our indices of quality, they do not fare better.

Characteristics of the Interorganizational Network

Of all of the variables about which we have information, the literature on the last set is most baffling. The desirability of "inside" versus "outside" evaluations has been constantly discussed. Moreover, the question of how and by whom decisions about the research should be made has been the subject of numerous debates. On the one side, there are those who assert that any evaluation that does not actively involve the action staff in determining and executing the research process is doomed to failure from the beginning. For one thing the action staff must be consulted in order to de-

Table 6.13. Academic Discipline and Other Correlates of Quality

Discipline	Grant	3 years +	University	Evaluation and Action in Same Organization	Formal Theoretical Framework	Academic Audience
Economics	−.28*	−.17†	−.12	−.15‡	−.15‡	−.21†
Psychology	.21†	.25*	.18*	.19†	.38*	.13‡
Sociology	−.04	−.06	.01	−.13	.03	−.01
Education	.01	.04	−.05	−.07	−.02	.01
Medicine, social work, psychiatry	.22*	.05	.15‡	.17†	−.08	.14‡
Other	−.11	−.06	−.15‡	−.14‡	−.18†	−.04

* = $p < .001$
† = $p < .01$
‡ = $p < .05$

termine how they define program success. As stated earlier, Freeman and Sherwood (1965), and Coleman (1969) posit that in order to specify program goals, means of goal attainment, processes by which means are implemented, and the like, the evaluation staff must do some intensive and extensive consultation with the action staff. There are those, however, who take the stance that sustained contact with an action-program staff diminishes scientific objectivity. The action staff is viewed as a seductress trying to tempt the scientist into commitment to service regardless of its effects.

We find that the characteristics of the interorganizational network explain 11 percent of the variance, significant at the .01 level. Interestingly, however, this set only explains 2 percent of the variance when the other sets of variables are taken into account. It is an important set of determinants mainly in its relationship to the other characteristics studied. Alone, this set of variables is not a strong correlate of research quality. Since organizational relations are a key concern in evaluation research, however, we will go into some detail on their relationships to quality. Table 6.14

Table 6.14. Organizational Arrangements and Research Quality

	Organizational Arrangements	
	---	---
Research Quality	(N = 62) Evaluation and Action Staffs Part of the Same Organization	(N = 90) Evaluation and Action Staffs of Different Organizations
High	27%	10%
Medium	37	28
Low	36	62

$\chi^2 = 12.64$, p $<.01$

indicates that when the evaluation and action staffs are part of the same organization, there is a higher percentage of studies doing relatively better research than when the evaluation and action staffs are in different organizations wherein there is a greater proportion among the less well-executed studies.

From Table 6.15, we conclude that it is advantageous to have the action and evaluation staffs make research decisions jointly. While the relationship is not statistically significant, the pattern is rather clear. Our data suggest that a greater degree of *interdependence* between the action and evaluation staffs is advantageous in order to minimize low-quality research. As shown in Table 6.16, there is a weak pattern of association between research quality and the relations between evaluation and funding-agency staff.

Table 6.15. Working Relations between the Evaluation and
Action Staffs and Research Quality

| | Working Relationship | | |
| | $(N = 67)$ | $(N = 35)$ | $(N = 50)$ |
Reseach Quality	Evaluation and Action Staffs Make Joint Research Decisions	Evaluation Staff Makes Research Decisions with Review by Action Staff	Evaluation Staff Makes Research Decisions Independent of Action Staff
High	25%	6%	14%
Medium	32	34	30
Low	43	60	56

$\chi^2 = 7.31$, p is not significant

Table 6.16. Working Relations between the Evaluation and Sponsoring-
Agency Staffs and Research Quality

| | Working Relationship | | | |
| | $(N = 13)$ | $(N = 32)$ | $(N = 67)$ | $(N = 72)$ |
Research Quality	Funding Agency Makes Research Decisions	Evaluation and Funding Agency Staffs Make Decisions Jointly	Evaluation Staff Makes Decisions with Review by Funding Agency	Evaluation Staff Makes Decisions Independent of Funding Agency
High	38%	22%	27%	25%
Medium	31	50	52	53
Low	31	28	21	22

$\chi^2 = 3.2$, p is not significant

Tables 6.17 and 6.18 show how each variable fares on quality. We can narrow down the most important variables to two: (1) organizational arrangements and (2) the working relationship between the evaluation and action staffs regarding research decisions. Since we know that these two variables are intercorrelated (see Table 3.7), what remains to be seen is how the relationship of the latter to research quality is affected when we control for one of them. We controlled for organizational arrangements since it is the stronger of the two variables. In Figure 6.1, it is shown that what is of prime importance is that the evaluation and action staffs be part of the same organization, since when they are in different organizations they seem to do less well in terms of research quality. If, however, they are in different organizations, it seems important that the staffs work jointly on making decisions about the research. Thus, our findings support the asser-

Table 6.17. Amount of Variance Explained by Working Relations

	Organizational Arrangements	Working Relationship between Evaluation and Action Staffs	Working Relationship between Evaluation and Funding-Agency Staff
Amount of variance explained	10%*	6%†	3%

* p = <.001
† p = <.01

Table 6.18. Organizational Characteristics and Research Quality

	Deviation from Overall Mean
Organizational Arrangements	
Evaluation and action in the same organization	+.6
Evaluation and action in different organizations	−.4
Working Relationship between Evaluation and Action Staffs	
Joint decisions	+.4
Evaluator's decisions reviewed by action staff	−.3
Evaluators make decisions independently	−.3
Working Relationship between Evaluation and Funding-Agency Staffs	
Evaluators make decisions independent of funding agency	+.2
Funding agency makes decisions	+.1
Evaluators make decisions with review by funding agency	—
Evaluation and funding-agency staffs make decisions jointly	−.5

tion of Freeman and Sherwood (1965), and Coleman (1969), that in order to execute an adequate evaluation study, the action staff must play a role in the research process as well.

CONCLUSIONS

In this chapter, our multivariate analyses have confirmed previous findings and pointed out that the same variables earlier identified one by one consistently show up as strong correlates of research quality when

Figure 6.1

Characteristics of the Interorganizational Network (Mean-Quality Scores)

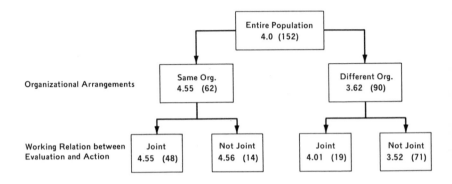

NOTE:
"Joint" refers to studies where the evaluation and action teams worked together in making decisions about the research plan.

"Not joint" refers to where the evaluators worked independently or had their decisions reviewed but the final judgments about the research plan were their own.

looked at together. The key variables are (1) the nature of the award, (2) the federal agency sponsoring the research, (3) the length of time allotted for the evaluation study, (4) the nature of the theoretical framework guiding the action program, (5) the type of organization with which the evaluator is affiliated, (6) the academic discipline of the project director, (7) the major audience to which research findings are addressed as defined by the evaluator, (8) the organizational arrangements between the evaluation and action components, and (9) the working relationship between the evaluation and action staffs with respect to decisions about the research. Some other variables conspicuously are not on this list, such as the amount of funds allocated or the highest earned degree. But it is clear that the polar types derived from examining the properties of the research enterprise—academic versus entrepreneurial—is a useful delineating dimension.

To arrive at our final model we began by entering the nine key variables identified above plus the variables (10) amount of funds allocated, (11) complexity of the evaluation study, and (12) working relationship between the evaluation and funding agency staff vis-à-vis research decisions, into a regression equation to determine just how much of the variation in research quality these twelve characteristics could explain. Despite the fact that we were encouraged in being able to account for 37 percent of the variance, we were displeased with having so many variables to work with in drawing up a final model. In order to reduce that number to a more workable set, we attempted to isolate the set of variables, fewest in number, which together would still account for a substantial amount of variation in research quality. Accordingly, we reduced our list to seven variables, plus the variable sponsoring agency, hoping to be able to eventually eliminate the sponsoring agency as a key correlate. Not that the sponsoring agency is by any means unimportant; rather, it is less manipulable in the sense of policy recommendations, and it would be to our advantage not to include it in a final model.

The seven variables selected were (1) nature of the award, (2) length of time for the evaluation, (3) nature of the theoretical framework, (4) type of organization, (5) major audience, (6) project director's academic discipline, and (7) organizational arrangements between the evaluation and action components. Regressing these variables on our index, we find that *together they account for 34 percent of the variance in research quality,* significant at the .001 level; adding in the variable "sponsoring agency" only raises that R^2 from .34 to .35. Clearly, the increment is small enough to warrant leaving that variable out of the final model.

Working with these seven key variables, the question next became whether their relationship to research quality is additive or whether there were some interaction effects, i.e., whether certain combinations of characteristics occurring simultaneously resulted in a greater or lesser research quality. Again using a regression analysis format, we tested for all interactions between each of these variables with every other variable. Our results indicate that only one of the possible 49 interaction effects (first-order interactions) is statistically significant. Since this finding could be due to chance alone and since there appears to be no substantive theoretical explanation, we shall proceed to present a final model which makes the assumption that there are no significant interaction effects operating.

The Final Model

A re-examination of Tables 6.2, 6.5, 6.8 and 6.17 lends support to the conclusion drawn above, i.e., that the seven characteristics noted are the correlates which best explain the variation we find in the quality of evaluation research. Importantly, however, none of these seven characteristics alone explains a substantial amount of variance when all other variables are controlled. This in no way diminishes their importance. Rather, it underscores once more the fact that these characteristics are intercorrelated. Table 6.19 shows the correlation among the characteristics of the entrepreneurial-type evaluations as well as the correlation of each to our index of research quality. Table 6.20 shows the same for academic-type evaluations.

Table 6.19. Correlation Matrix of Entrepreneurial-Type Characteristics and Research Quality

	Contract	1–1½ Years	Profit Corp.	Economist	Non-Academic Audience	Social Service Model	Evaluation & Action in Different Organizations	Overall Research Quality
Contract	—	.15‡	.47*	.28*	.35*	.15	.45*	−.38*
12–18 months		—	.18‡	.09	.08	−.02	.12	−.29*
Profit Corp.			—	.20*	.28*	.12	.36*	−.19‡
Economist				—	.21†	.06	.15*	−.11
Non-Academic Audience					—	.06	.26*	−.27*
Social Service Model						—	.15*	−.09
Evaluation and Action Different Organizations							—	−.30*

* = p <.001
† = p <.01
‡ = p <.05

Table 6.20. Correlation Matrix of Academic-Type Characteristics and Research Quality

	Grant	3 Years +	University or University Affiliate	Psychol- ogist	Academic Audience	Formal Theoretical Framework	Evaluation and Action Part of Same Organization	Overall Research Quality
Grant	—	.13‡	.18†	.17†	.21†	.29*	.17†	+.38*
3 years+		—	.19†	.24*	.26*	.45*	.26*	+.30*
University or university affiliate			—	.38*	.13‡	.21†	.25*	+.22†
Psychologist				—	.24*	.25*	.27*	+.36*
Academic audience					—	.35*	.35*	+.27*
Formal theoretical framework						—	.26*	+.32*
Evaluation and action part of same organization							—	+.30*

* p < .001
† p < .01
‡ p < .05

In order to compare these two model types on research quality, we compute predicted mean scores for each based on the final regression equation model. Table 6.21 presents the regression equation, Table 6.22 the predicted mean score for "academic"-type evaluations, and Table 6.23 the predicted mean score for "entrepreneurial"-type evaluations.

While these are predicted mean scores and therefore limited in terms of generalizability, it is interesting to note that for "academic-type" evaluations, the predicted score is 5.88. The implication is that this type evaluation is likely to result in research studies which adhere almost perfectly to basic methodological prescriptions. Thus, Table 6.22 provides a further basis for concluding that *academic-type evaluations are likely to be of high quality.*

The predicted mean for "entrepreneurial-type" evaluations is equal

Table 6.21. The Final Equation

$$Y = 4.44 + (-.71D_4) - (.01D_{12} + 1.00D_{13} + .18D_{14} + .22D_{15})$$
$$+ (.41D_{25} + .33D_{26} + .56D_{27}) + (.23D_{29}) + (.20D_{35} + .46D_{36})$$
$$- .29D_{37} - .15D_{38} - .59D_{39}) + (-.74D_{65} - .44D_{66}) + (.19D_{68})$$

Award	D_4 = a contract
Years of Study	D_{12} = less than 1 year
	D_{13} = 1–1½ years
	D_{14} = 1½–2 years
	D_{15} = 2–3 years
Type of Organization	D_{25} = Profit Corporation
	D_{26} = Non-Profit
	D_{27} = Educational Institution
Organizational Arrangements	D_{29} = "Inside" Evaluation
Academic Discipline of Project Director	D_{35} = Economics
	D_{36} = Psychology
	D_{37} = Sociology
	D_{38} = Education
	D_{39} = Medicine/Psychiatry/Social Work
Nature of Theoretical Framework	D_{65} = No Theory
	D_{66} = Social Service Model
Major Audience	D_{68} = Academic

(Any response category not listed is equal to zero for the purpose of computation. They represent "left out" categories. "Left out" categories refer to the category in dummy variable regression for which no dummy was entered into the equation. See Cohen [1968] for a more in-depth explanation of the dummy variable regression format.)

Table 6.22. Predicted Mean Score for Academic-Type Evaluations

Characteristics		From Table 6.21
Nature of Award:	Grant	.00
Length of Study (years):	3 years+	.00
Type of Organization	Educational Institutions	+.56
Project Director's Academic Discipline:	Psychology	+.46
Major Audience:	Academic	+.19
Nature of Theoretical Framework:	Formal Theoretical Model	.00
Organizational Arrangements:	Evaluation and Action Groups in the Same Organization	+.23
		$Y = 4.44 + 1.44$

Table 6.23. Predicted Mean Score for Entrepreneurial-Type Evaluations

Characteristics		From Table 6.21
Nature of Award:	Contract	−.71
Length of Study (years):	1–1½ years	−1.00
Type of Organization:	Profit	+.41
Project Director's Academic Discipline:	Economics	+.20
Major Audience:	Non-Academic	.00
Nature of Theoretical Framework:	Social Service Model	−.44
Organizational Arrangements:	Evaluation and Action in Different Organizations	.00
		$Y = 4.44 − 1.54$

to 2.90. This finding reconfirms the conclusion drawn earlier, i.e., "entrepreneurial-type" evaluations are likely to result in research studies which fail to adhere to basic methodological prescriptions. Moreover, in comparing the predicted mean of 2.90 to 5.88, we are strengthened in our contention that *entrepreneurial-type evaluations are likely to result in research of lesser quality.*

The final task is to make our findings useful, for they cannot be left simply to sit. To end our study here would be to have conducted merely another academic inquiry, and our contribution would be useful primarily to a small audience of colleagues and researchers. Our purpose in doing this study, as we stated at the outset, was to contribute to the state of the art of evaluation research. Toward this end, our final chapter.

CHAPTER SEVEN
Recommendations for a National Policy

From the standpoint of research quality, there is an obvious solution for improving evaluation research: have all studies undertaken in academic research centers, by Ph.D. psychology professors and those with similar training and orientation, include a commitment that the research results must be published in refereed social science journals, provide funds only as grants and have them awarded on the basis of peer-review committee judgments, allow a time period of from three to five years for the planning and conduct of the research, have the grants monitored by federal officials with a high degree of social-science graduate training and with reference groups consisting of academic researchers, and insist on the research being undertaken in collaboration with the action agency.

In brief, one alternative is to expand evaluation-research activities that have the properties of what we have termed the academic type and decrease the support of the polar, entrepreneurial type. Certainly there are limitations to the design of our study, and to the indicators of quality of evaluation research. But we feel that we have made a convincing case, consistent with ideas and empirical findings about the general scientific-research enterprise, that if high-quality research is the goal, the conditions of academic research are required; and certainly there is no question that quality is critical in evaluation research. But, at the same time, it is foolish to argue for the solution suggested in the opening paragraph, from the standpoint of national needs, political practicalities, and the existing posture of the academic establishment.

135

First, as Coleman (1973) had indicated, research for policy purposes remains an idle aspiration if the findings are not available when needed for political decision-making. Well-designed and carefully executed studies are worthless if they do not precede the political decision-making process. Completed research of more questionable quality—or none at all—will be the basis for policy determination, since neither policy-makers in the executive branch, human-resource administrators and planners, nor congressional groups are likely to be patient and await the deliberations of professors in the face of interest-group pressure and propitious opportunities to innovate in the human-resource area.

Second, turning evaluation research back to the social science academy presumes that university-based social scientists will accept the responsibility of studying matters of national priority, and engage in the necessary contractual negotiations and program-design relationships. Some do now of course, but many of the comments offered on the sociology of science in the last chapter contradict the idea that the values and concerns of the majority of academic investigators, as well as their style of operations, can be modified sufficiently so that they fit into the undertaking of research carried out as part of a political process.

Third, there is the evaluation-research industry. A large number of organizations, profit-making groups, independent semiacademic nonprofit centers, as well as university-based investigators have a major investment in undertaking evaluation studies. After all, unless the trajectory changes, it will soon be a 100 million dollar industry. It is unrealistic to believe that eliminating the participation of all but academic groups is possible, for we know that much less extreme reshaping of political and economic structures in the United States is for all practical purposes impossible to imagine.

Finally, despite numerous criticisms and efforts to modify the existing civil-service and political-appointee systems of federal agencies and executive departments, it appears relatively hopeless to restructure the entire bureaucracy. While we have emphasized the need for evaluation research in the human-services and resource areas, the various federal groups have other functions—their leadership and most of their "middle-management" cannot be expected to have the training and time, let alone the commitment, to initiate, monitor, and promote studies of outstanding quality. Their jobs are bigger than evaluation research, and they must get them done. Lower-level personnel with requisite training and outlook are difficult to attract and retain, even by the most academically and scientifically oriented agencies.

Thus, as self-seeking and tempting as it is for us to take the position that evaluation research should be predominantly an academic enterprise, this solution must be rejected. There is somewhat of a parallel in the field of medicine that is a warning of possible consequences, if one were to opt for this solution. The now classic Flexner investigation of the early 1900s eliminated many of the entrepreneurial and proprietary activities in medical education, and returned training in medicine to the university, and much of medical care to the academically oriented hospital. The reasoning was not much different from that elaborated in Chapter 6. But the consequences today certainly must be questioned: for the results of overemphasizing the academic aspects of medicine account in part for the shortage of physicians, particularly general practitioners; the power of organized medicine, both at a local and international level; and the rigidity of the medical-care system that impedes efforts to change the ways services are delivered and medicine practiced.

In brief, if evaluation research is to prosper as an activity of social worth, if it is to contribute to the design and implementation of innovative programs and social-action efforts designed to modify the human condition, a solution must be found that is both consistent with the purposes and potential utility of evaluation research. Such a solution, we believe, cannot be a piecemeal change in the way federal agencies go about their business and the procedures by which contracts and grants are provided and modified. Moreover, a few changes within evaluation research organizations are not sufficient. What is needed is a national evaluation policy: major changes in the federal structure that surrounds evaluation-research activities are required, as well as parallel modifications in research organizations—ones that will have an impact on how evaluation research is undertaken—which will then maximize the utility and the political process by which programs are initiated, modified, and extended.

It is not simply the considerable costs with limited payoff of current evaluation efforts that suggest the urgency of a national policy. Rather, it is extensive costs of human-welfare programs and their limited efficacy in remedying the myriad of social and interpersonal problems that confront community members at the present time that calls for timely, rigorous evaluation research. What is required are changes of an extensive nature in the evaluation research endeavor; unless an intensive effort is made to modify the existing situation, evaluation research will remain a rational approach to policy and program planning that fails to contribute much to the development of federal human-resource programs.

TIMING OF STUDIES

Most social science investigators are well aware not only of the need for fairly extensive periods of time in order to undertake high-quality research, but also of the difficulty of predicting with precision the termination date of studies. At the same time, it bears repeated emphasis that evaluation research represents a valuable input into the decision-making process at the federal level only when findings are available prior to the need to develop policy. Perhaps the most critical need is to organize evaluation-research studies in ways that maximize the possibility of findings being available earlier than the complicated process of deciding on programs within the federal establishment. This indeed represents a challenge both for investigators and funding agencies.

The Need for an Intelligence System

Perhaps the idea is simplistic, but the most facile way of making evaluation studies available, at the appropriate time, is to anticipate the policies and programs that will be considered at a federal level in the future. This simply is not done very often now. Most of the extensive federal programs, whether they be experimental efforts in education, the guaranteed annual wage in welfare, or new means of providing housing for the nation's poor do not come off the drawing boards instantaneously. Rather, the history of most programs that have been adopted in, say, the last five years probably goes back a decade or more. But presently, little is done to anticipate evaluation-research needs in advance.

At the same time that the federal establishment makes efforts domestically and internationally to predict a wide variety of actions, and similar projections are commonplace in the economic and industrial sectors of the United States, there currently is little work being undertaken on anticipating the future within the human-resource area. It is absolutely critical that the federal establishment begin now to project programs that may be at the top of the political priority list in the 1980s, and immediately begin demonstration and action experiments with proper evaluation on them.

What this means essentially is mounting a continual series of social experiments, with the full knowledge and awareness that only a percentage—perhaps a relatively small percentage—of them will have direct relevance later to the political decision-making process. Many admittedly would be conducted and "stored," because predictions and speculations on the direction of policy and program development were erroneous. Naturally, research on better means for predicting and projecting the future in federal programs could increase the batting average. Support of research for developing better techniques of predicting future program directions in the human-resource area is an obvious need.

But even if only a small proportion of evaluation research projects that begin "on speculation" fed relevant information into the decision-making process, it would be worth it. "Anticipatory" evaluation projects mounted at the $150,000 to $250,000 level are not an excess use of funds, even if ten or twenty or fifty such efforts are initiated per year with the full knowledge that perhaps two or three or five of them are going to feed directly into the political process. It clearly is not a foolish idea considering the extensive costs of most social-action programs that are eventually adopted on a national basis.

Further, such a planned effort on the part of the federal establishment would provide a storehouse of information on the implementation and impact of various action and intervention approaches. Such a bank of information would be a catalyst to program planners and policy-makers in the future regarding the design of programs; it would accelerate movement in the direction of becoming an "experimenting society." When one considers the price tag on most human-resource programs conducted on a nationwide basis, and the costs and effort expended in groping and searching for new ideas, even if expenditures for such purposes were in the range of 30 to 50 million dollars per annum, the cost could be justified and defended. It would take only one or two wiser decisions regarding implantation of national programs per year in order to compensate for the cost of early intelligence efforts and anticipatory high-quality evaluation research of the range of programs that have a plausible chance of national adoption. There are, it should be pointed out, only a finite number of innovations that are possible, and thus eventually what would accrue is a body of findings and propositions that could readily be made available when there are changes in philosophy, administration, and viewpoint regarding what should be done to improve the human condition.

Distribution of Responsibilities

Any implantation of the notion of developing an effective intelligence system as early as possible, and supporting the evaluation of programs that are highly tentative, requires a reallocation of responsibilities for evaluation research within the federal establishment. We do not believe, in general, that the individual executive departments—whose responsibilities are centered around the day-to-day activities in the human-services and human-resource area and who, to a large extent, are responsive to, rather than innovative in, program development—represent the best loci for early intelligence and anticipatory evaluation activities. Particularly doubtful, in our minds, is the notion that lower level federal groups who have an investment and a stake in existing programs and ideas that have sprung from their loins and those of their constituencies are in the best position to undertake such efforts. Rather, we would recommend that these evaluation efforts be the province and responsibility of groups that are close to the highest levels of political decision-making. Thus, for example, we would recommend that early intelligence systems and evaluations that are conceived and initiated prior to their being firm ideas in the political arena be in the hands of the Office of Management and Budget and the General Accounting Office. At the present time, neither of these two groups are active in the process of early intelligence, nor do they have either the funding or the structure and staff to sponsor regularly experimental evaluation studies on their own and to feed research results to the leadership of the executive branch and Congress.

We propose that automatically each year perhaps 1 to 2 percent of the federal budget for programs on the human condition be allocated to these two groups so that they may carry on the noted functions. Both groups should be required to set up the necessary administrative machinery and apparatus in order to undertake these tasks. At the present time, if they are involved at all, it is in retrospectively judging the results of evaluation research and occasionally trying to influence other parts of the federal establishment to undertake evaluation studies. Both the executive branch and the congressional one require organizations which can undertake studies early, with sufficient time to feed the results into the highest levels of political decision-making.

Developing Evaluation Models

Another way of speeding up the time of studies would be to develop evaluation-research modules that could be fitted together in the design of studies, rather than more or less designing each study fresh as if no work had gone on in the same or related areas. For example, inspection of evaluation-research studies in education show that there are virtually an endless series of outcome criteria used to measure impact. Not only does this water down the opportunities to make comparisons between different types of innovative programs—the criteria used to determine outcome are different —but each study begins more or less with criteria and instrument-development processes that are time-consuming and, under the pressures of day-to-day work, often not accomplished well. The same is true of various techniques to measure process: virtually all evaluation studies being conducted now employ their own specific methods and means of analysis in trying to ascertain whether or not programs are undertaken in ways consistent with program objectives.

It would be a mistake, of course, to insist that only prior-conceived modules constitute the design elements in evaluation studies. But much time and effort could be saved if there were a finite set of methods and criteria, as well as analysis procedures, that were regarded as important implements in the various investigations conducted in specific a:eas and fields. Additional new and novel approaches for assessing impact and process could be included as well, of course, in the design of individual studies. But the need for accumulation of results and speed of work suggest that "prepackaging" is a critical area for attention. It is a place where academicians and university-research groups could make important contributions. It implies, for example, the development of standardized measures of delinquent behavior, of psychotherapeutic outcome, and of successful work careers. It further implies that in particular kinds of evaluation studies, parallel methods of data collection and analysis should be used routinely in order to measure process. Undoubtedly, much resistance will be found among the more academic researchers, who may regard it as a restriction of their investigative freedom. But, as repeatedly noted, evaluation research primarily should be conducted for policy purposes and for political purposes, and thus some sacrifice of individuality is necessary because of time demands and the urgency of being able to compare results of evaluation studies.

SPONSORING EVALUATION RESEARCH

As Wholey and associates (1970) have noted, part of the problem of the award of grants and contracts is the lack of specificity and soundness in requests for research proposals that are made by federal agencies. We found in this study that peer-reviewed grants tend to be of higher quality than evaluation research funded by competitive bid contracts. But it should be noted that we do not advocate sitting back and waiting until creditable proposals are offered by academic persons who are primarily concerned with studying their own interests. Rather, a number of interrelated procedures need to be developed in order to maximize the benefits in terms of the quality of research that seems to accrue to peer-group selection of well-conceived proposals.

Writing Specifications

We think it is simply unrealistic to expect the typical administrator or contract officer to have the know-how to write specifications for evaluation research that are concise and detailed, and to which the research community can respond. Rather, we would insist that requests for proposals must be so clear and complete that, at least in broad detail, they are pretty much the completed designs for studies.

Since it is unlikely that this will occur often within the federal establishment by regular, full-time staff, we propose that either selected groups of researchers, such as are found in the major universities, or regularly constituted panels of consultants be responsible for the explication of research specifications. Some of the very best researchers in universities and related centers, who might be unwilling to devote a major portion of their time on a continuing basis to evaluations may be interested in such a role, bringing them into the evaluation-research orbit. This would admittedly increase the costs of investigations and reduce somewhat the influence of the regular cadre within the federal establishment. But it would provide a more definitive yardstick upon which to appraise submitted proposals. Moreover, if the specifications were appropriately written, it is at least a reasonable hypothesis that a larger number of more competent organizations would risk the time, trouble, and expense to bid for contracts.

Peer Review

We believe it is critical that judgments on the awarding of funds should not be made primarily by persons within the federal establishment. It is possible to extend the peer-review system to virtually all evaluation contracts as well as researcher-initiated grants. To a considerable extent, agencies like the National Institute of Mental Health have extended the peer-review system to the letting of contracts as well. Doing this requires implementing the model of a study section that is commonly employed in the National Institutes of Health and Mental Health. Such study sections should have the services of an executive secretary, who, as much as possible, should be the peer of the study-section members. He or she must be an individual with a considerable degree of expertise and training and be provided with sufficient authority and funding to undertake and arrange site visits for the study-section members, hold sufficient meetings and face-to-face contacts to consider proposals carefully, and to facilitate and enhance an ambience of concern with the quality of the work undertaken.

It should be pointed out that, like the proper development of specifications, the use of peer reviews would increase federal costs for evaluations. But it may not increase the net cost to the government, for clearly some contracts are now let and some research is undertaken that is simply impossible to do with enough rigor and quality to make them worthwhile from the outset. A number of the larger studies we reviewed, and others that have come to our attention in the course of doing this research, would simply not have been attempted or would have been attempted in a different way on a different scale if the process of funding was more of a "professional" and substantive rather than a formalistic and procedural effort.

Responsibility for Funding

One of the surprising findings of both Wholey et al. (1970) and ourselves is that, for the most part, funds for evaluation research are located fairly low down in the various federal departments and are usually not regularly expended by such key groups as the Office of Management and

Budget and the General Accounting Office. As noted, we believe this is a mistake. In the first place, it means that perhaps six to eight and as many as twelve different groups in such departments as Health, Education and Welfare have staff involved in developing contract specifications. They often do not have a high enough individual volume to maintain the peer-review committee system that we advocate as the major, indeed exclusive, way of making awards.

Moreover, many of the agencies that do make the awards—subagencies of the federal departments—simply do not have an orientation toward research since often it is not a major operation compared with program activities. Finally, many agencies have an investment in demonstrating or not demonstrating the utility of particularly innovative efforts. Sometimes their interest in carrying out evaluation research is essentially responsive to either pressure at a higher level in the federal executive agencies or the urgings of the legislative branch and occasional congressional legislation.

Thus, except in the cases of those agencies such as NIMH that undertake high volumes of evaluation research and do so with a fairly neutral stance and a commitment to evaluation, we recommend that responsibility for evaluation efforts in each executive department be lodged in the Secretary's office. The results of evaluation research become critical for a decision-making process that emanates from their offices. Yet, currently, for all practical purposes, persons at the Secretary's level have too modest funds and inadequate staffs available for evaluation opportunities. Funding for the various executive branches should include a small percentage, say 1 or 2 percent of their total operations, to be expended for evaluation research. Responsibility for all or most evaluation research should be given to either one of the assistant secretaries (or a new assistant secretary) with the necessary apparatus and resources for producing concise and detailed specifications and for establishing and maintaining necessary peer-review committees that make the decisions on the awarding of grants and contracts. Since our study, at least in HEW, the Secretary's office has taken a much more active role in evaluation research activities, although a less strong one than we feel is desirable.

Reviewing Funding Arrangements

We propose further that not only is it essential that better specifications be the rule, peer review the means of selection, and responsibility lodged at a high level for evaluation-research activities, but the entire process should be subjected to outside scrutiny. We recommend that a group of well-trained evaluation researchers serve term appointments, under the sponsorship of either the Office of Management and Budget or the General

Accounting Office to carefully and continually analyze the process by which evaluation research is funded. Indeed, we feel that these groups should have a more expanded role in the evaluation endeavor than they see for themselves even at the present time. While it may not be possible to scrutinize every award in depth, certainly the larger ones and a sample of the others could be subjected to careful review. Responsible officials in the various agencies should have feedback on the way their award process is being conducted from this commission. For such a commission to perform that task prior to the awarding of funds may be unwieldy and jeopardize the lead time required for studies. But clearly, such a retrospective effort would do much to make certain that the award process is well developed, well administered, and conducted as carefuly and appropriately as possible.

Multiple Evaluations

In certain cases, where programs are of extreme national importance and when anticipated expenditures for programs are extensive, we recommend multiple evaluations. It seems foolhardy, for example, to examine sweeping innovations in health care, education, and welfare services by contracting only one evaluation research group to undertake a relatively confined investigation. There are instances where multiple evaluations are taking place under somewhat varied conditions. Perhaps the most striking current efforts along these lines are the several experiments being conducted by the Office of Economic Opportunity to determine the outcome of a guaranteed annual wage on work activity and employment seeking. There are other illustrations of multiple evaluations being done, such as the several contracts let by the National Institute of Education to study the impact of the experimental school program.

But multiple evaluations are rare. In most cases, moreover, with the partial exception of the guaranteed annual wage experiments, the procedures and criteria employed are so markedly different that it is not possible to compare the results of the several evaluations. We are proposing that there be multiple evaluations with either the same outcome or an overlapping set of criteria, and the assumption that the methodological procedures employed in the two or more evaluations meet the required standards of quality. There are a number of federal programs that consume millions of dollars of taxpayers' funds which merit multiple assessments.

Such multiple assessments also would be an invaluable learning experience with respect to the conduct of evaluation research. Evaluations that were done by persons in different disciplines conducted in different organizations certainly could provide information on how one might improve the state of the art.

THE MONITORING PROCESS

For the most part, the monitoring process of federal agencies is conducted by internal staff. As noted at the outset of this volume, monitoring ranges from formal scrutiny of accounting records to continued collaboration between the staff of the federal agencies and the evaluation groups. Monitoring may be more superficial than is desirable for several reasons. First, many federal groups simply lack persons with a high degree of technical training and research experience who can delve into various projects with the necessary expertise. Second, those who do the monitoring in federal agencies often are viewed with suspicion and degradation, particularly when the evaluation research is undertaken by academically oriented groups. We believe that some fundamental modifications are essential in the style of monitoring evaluation research studies.

Employing Nonfederal Monitors

For the most part, we believe that continued detailed and technically sensitive monitoring cannot be undertaken by persons within the federal establishment. Rather, we would propose that highly trained and experienced individuals should, preferably through the organizations with which they are affiliated, be employed on a contractual-grant basis to monitor projects in particular areas. We believe this would be another useful tool for academically affiliated groups of evaluation researchers. It would allow them opportunities to participate in a public-service activity without becoming overwhelmed by full-time commitments to a large number of evaluation studies. One inducement for academically oriented groups to undertake this role could be fairly generous financial arrangements with them, so that taking on this responsibility provided some relatively free funds for student training and basic work in the evaluation-research field. Again, like the support of evaluation research, persons and organizations selected for this role should be chosen on a peer-review basis.

Audit of Evaluation Research

We believe that it is the responsibility of the federal government, possibly through the Behavioral Sciences Division of the National Academy of Science, to undertake annually an analysis of evaluation-research studies supported by the federal government and to prepare a critique of the research methods employed. While we have no particular brief for either the instruments or methodology used in our study, we would suggest that some procedure—working from more finely developed research proposals, reports of investigators, face-to-face confrontation with evaluation researchers, or some combination of approaches—should be used each year to review studies; then, a public document that describes the range of work, costs, methods employed, utility of results, and prospects for improving the field should be published.

Such a retrospective effort would not be unduly expensive. The study reported here cost less than the average of the several hundred evaluation studies that we reviewed for fiscal 1970. But it is fairly certain that making such a public review each year would be one way of increasing the visibility that we believe is an important social-control mechanism for the evaluation-research industry.

Evaluation of Evaluations

Russell Sage Foundation (1974), as part of its program to improve the state of the art in evaluation research, provided funds for three different groups to review three major social-action experiments. In many ways this was a valuable exercise, not only in terms of substantial returns through the reanalysis of data, but also by obtaining insights into the social and political processes involved in evaluation research. At this point, we believe that extensive case-by-case "evaluations of evaluations" are both expensive and unwieldy to conduct. However, we recommend that a small committee, preferably supported by nongovernmental funds, be brought into existence to scrutinize carefully some of the proposals and reports of evaluation groups. Such a committee could arrange for serious critiques of completed studies, and could make these critiques available and distribute them to a variety of persons in government and the evaluation-research industry. Again, while this may be viewed as an impertinent invasion of a relationship between a research group and a sponsor, we believe it is essential in order to maximize opportunities to make the proposals, procedures, and results of evaluation research visible to a wide audience. Again, it would function as a social control mechanism and a motivation for evaluation researchers to excel in the quality of their work.

Publication Requirements

For the most part, evaluation-research studies, particularly those done as contracts, are not published and widely distributed. Sometimes this is a function of the particular federal agency, which fails to encourage publication; at other times it is a lack of interest on the part of evaluation-research organizations. Like the other efforts suggested for monitoring, we believe that a means to maximize visibility is a key way of improving the quality of evaluation research. Several different proposals may be entertained. A requirement could be imposed on evaluation-research organizations that all their work must be available in either commercially distributed monographs or articles in high-quality journals. An alternative commitment would be for the federal government to put out, quarterly or biannually, a journal-type publication that reported completed studies and in some cases detailed progress reports. It should be a federal publication with standards similar to those that exist in high-quality journals in the social science field. Finally, at least one nonprofit independent research institute gives a small bonus to their staff for each paper published in a refereed journal as an incentive to their investigators to publish. More groups should do so.

Rating Evaluation-Research Organizations

The number of different groups and different types of groups that conduct evaluation research is fairly large. However, at the present time there does not exist, at least when the contract mechanisms are employed, the same type of dossier on evaluation-research organizations and their staffs that is available under the competitive grant processes of such agencies as NIH and NIMH. We believe it is important that the federal government have available, at the time of judging proposed work, a history of the investigators and their organization. There should be summaries of any actions, positive and negative, in terms of past efforts to receive support of agencies, professional reactions to completed work, and so on, available to the proposed peer-review groups when they decide on a particular organization for an evaluation-research award. In our preliminary efforts, when we searched the files of most of the agencies who use contract procedures, there was usually only superficial *pro forma* information about the organizations selected and rejected to undertake the evaluation studies.

THE EVALUATION-RESEARCH ENTERPRISE

The major thrust of the recommendations up to now have been on the remolding of the ways that federal agencies plan, initiate, and monitor evaluation-research studies. We have recommended increased participation by two key government agencies, the Office of Management and Budget and the General Accounting Office. Further, we have suggested that additional responsibilities be assumed by the various offices of the secretaries of the executive departments. Finally, we have indicated the importance of increasing the participation of nongovernmental persons at all points in the course of an evaluation-research effort on the grounds that neither the existing structure, which places the responsibility for implementation of evaluation studies at the level of the operating agencies within the various departments, nor the talent available in these units are congruent with the sensitive, complex, and technically difficult aspects of developing, supporting, and monitoring evaluation-research efforts.

But in the end, unless the evaluation research endeavor is markedly different from other scientific study—which we do not believe is the case—the quality and utility of evaluation studies depends upon the persons who do the work, although the federal bureaucracy can take a number of important steps that would improve the quality of research. The current posture and workings of evaluation-research organizations must be modified as well, and the proposition is a simple one. Evaluation research will improve in quality if the persons and organizations doing the work internalize the norms that surround the activities of academically oriented scientists. It is what might be described as the professionalization of the evaluation-research enterprise that is required.

There are some trends in this direction even now. For example, a new journal, *Evaluation,* established with NIMH support, provides a forum for discussing, considering, and reporting results of evaluation studies. Further, commissions and committees, such as the 1971–1972 committee on evaluation research of the Social Science Research Council, provide opportunities for communication, exchange of views, and the development of practices and procedures for evaluation research; so too do the programs of various academic associations and professional groups of planners and applied research investigators.

This is not a new problem. An interesting analogy is the professionalization of public-opinion researchers. The past two decades have witnessed a marked growth in the academic orientation of persons in this field. The annual meetings of the American Association for Public Opinion Research as well as their journal, *Public Opinion Quarterly,* are forums in which persons who undertake studies of various sorts can communicate and exchange ideas. Further, they are means by which researchers are socialized to the importance of technical astuteness, and the critical need for constantly improving the craft and the methodological and conceptual underpinnings of public-opinion investigations.

The public-opinion field is mentioned here because it shares some of the same variegations of constituency as the evaluation-research enterprise. Persons who undertake public-opinion studies range from those affiliated with advertising companies and market-research groups, who are fundamentally concerned with the entrepreneurial gains from their work, to individuals whose primary affiliations are academic and who by topic and problem foci are interested in vastly different types of research activities. But, nevertheless, this is a field where there is at least some degree of shared communality of interest and research stance between groups who have some fundamentally different aspirations and motivations for their work.

The collaborative efforts of persons in operational research and the

computer sciences are other relevant analogies. Here too, despite dispari-
ties of interests, strides have been taken to develop an identity and an
orientation that is shared by persons regardless of their affiliations and motives for undertaking their work. Eventually, we would suppose the trajectory in the evaluation-research area will mirror those of the groups just
discussed. The issue is whether or not efforts can be undertaken to speed
up and maximize the possibilities of developing a shared value system and
an outlook that produces high-quality evaluation research more often than
seems to be the case now.

Developing an Organizational Identity

Most social researchers are often dismayed by the plethora of formal
professional organizations that spring up and persist. But they do function
to provide opportunities for communication and exchange of ideas, as well
as a common sense of identity for individuals engaged in similar work. As
we have documented, individuals in the evaluation-research enterprise
range in their basic academic disciplines from the social sciences to such
fields as public health, social work, and the like. Further, they vary in the
extent of formal academic training and the relevance of their educational
careers for the tasks that they perform. For all in the field and particularly
for those in profit-making groups, it would be exceedingly valuable if there
were a national organization of evaluation researchers. Such a group not
only could provide a forum through meetings and possibly publication of
one or more journals, but it could deal effectively with such matters as
ethics, future manpower needs, and relations between sponsors and researchers in the field. It would clearly increase the common grounds of persons heterogeneous in background and purpose.

Training for Evaluation Research

One of our underlying propositions is that there are a number of basic
research operations that characterize sound evaluation studies. In the past
several years, with support of federal agencies, several specialized graduate
programs in evaluation research have been started. The funding has generally come from health-related federal groups. These efforts have been
aborted to a large extent, however, by current government policy which
severely limits funds to universities for graduate fellowships and related
support of professors and activities. The blanket restriction of funds on the
grounds of a sufficient supply of social researchers has come at a time when
the existing supply of manpower for university teaching and basic research
activities has begun to reach relatively adequate levels. Under these circumstances, the opportunity exists to attract young, bright, energetic social

science students into areas such as evaluation research. The talent pool is there; however, the temptation to work in an activity in which there continues to be considerable opportunity for career development is dampened by a policy that does not allow taking advantage of student availability via graduate training programs to produce persons who are well-grounded both conceptually and methodologically, and who could join both profit and nonprofit evaluation-research groups.

But training in terms of the long-term graduate programs is only one remedy to the existing situation. Another is the implementation of short-term courses and on-the-job educational opportunities. Admittedly, a considerable amount of what takes place in evaluation research is learned only by doing. But this is not strictly the case. We propose that all evaluation-research groups who bid for contracts and grants must include in their proposals statements of ongoing and projected training programs for persons within their organizations. These might range from special short-term courses on an in-house basis to prolonged study leaves for individuals in order to increase their armamentarium for evaluation-research activities.

Developing Performance Standards

Earlier we suggested it is important that sponsoring federal agencies, from the initial point of contract and grant offerings, be concise, specific, and detailed about what is expected from evaluation-research groups in any particular investigation. At the same time, we think it important to encourage the diverse organizations in the evaluation-research enterprise to develop their own sets of performance standards and to collectively scrutinize their research efforts. Unless such collective action is possible, it is essential that federal sponsoring agencies employ strong sanctions in order to make certain that efforts are of sound quality. Rather than seeing the federal establishment move to a system of requiring bonds or engaging in legal action to recover poorly spent research funds, we believe that concerted, collective action of participants in research endeavors is a more appropriate solution. The development of performance standards does, however, require formal organizational relationships between various groups in the field.

Role of the Universities

University groups and individual academicians should be encouraged to relate more closely and continually to the independent nonprofit and the profit-making sectors of the evaluation enterprise. This is a responsibility we feel is generally ignored by the academic social science community. While most social scientists and their students today verbally acknowledge their responsibility to participate in efforts to improve the human condition, many do very little about it. Throughout the entire evaluation-research enterprise, there are many opportunities to develop intern and residency programs analogous to what takes place in medicine and such areas as clinical psychology.

Intern and residency programs are costly and time-consuming for universities, as well as for the research groups involved. But in the same way as it is generally acknowledged that teaching hospitals provide high-quality medical care, teaching-research organizations similarly should be able to undertake research of higher quality. Not only would we propose formal relationships between independent nonprofit groups and profit-making ones, with various social science departments that provide the training for evaluation researchers, but we would suggest that funds for such purposes be routinely provided as part of evaluation-research grants and contracts—if not as independent allocations to groups making such arrangements. Further we contend that the presence of well-supervised intern and residency programs for persons at various levels of training, ranging from the B.A. through the postdoctoral person, should be an important criterion in the award of evaluation research supported by federal agencies.

It is time, we believe, that social science research groups lessen their aloofness to the various types of organizations that undertake evaluation research and strenuously begin to initiate collaborative training efforts of the type noted. The reason is not solely the self-interests of evaluation-research organizations, but also an important means of maintaining the growth and development of the social sciences themselves. It is clear, although there is debate about the numbers and slopes of the trends, that opportunities in strictly academic types of activities for social sciences will be minimal for the next decade or so. At the same time, interest among students in the social sciences is high and the number of trained persons has increased. Collaborative arrangements with groups closer to the firing line in the evaluation-research enterprise is a solution to the possible overproduction and oversupply of social scientists that is often lamented.

Finally, university groups should be encouraged to continue and expand their interest in evaluation-research endeavors. In addition to actively competing for evaluation-research studies, they should promote, seek, and receive federal support in order to be able to undertake the fundamental and basic work of a methodological and conceptual sort that will permit higher-quality research. There are a number of possible ways of doing this. Resistance of academic groups to undertaking evaluation-research projects, we believe, would be lessened if the federal government could make commitments to provide a percentage of "free money" as an inducement to participate more actively in the area. While only a few well-established social scientists are willing to devote their full time for say two or three years to a particular project in which they have but minimal substantive interest, the enticement of supplementary funds for their personal work and for the educational and research programs of their departments would make such participation much more probable. Particularly in these times, well-trained, competent academicians are realistic or at least should be, in the face of declining training and research support.

CONCLUDING COMMENT

Several points made earlier in this document bear repeating. First, it is important to emphasize our commitment to evaluation research as a means of developing rational social policies and improving human-resource programs across a variety of areas. We are not suggesting the endeavor be downgraded because of current deficiencies. Along these lines, it should be noted that virtually all the projects that we identified and reviewed are concerned with what might be called innovative or modified program activity. We believe that the potential for evaluation research exists not only in assessing new and experimental efforts but should be a continual activity with respect to established federal programs. Along the same lines, while we have examined only programs directly supported by the federal establishment, there are an extensive number of social-action activities that are conducted at the state and local level, in which federal funds are only indirectly involved or not involved at all. These, too, merit the application of evaluation-research inquiry.

Second, we are of the opinion that fragmented efforts, that is, the adoption of one or two of our recommendations, are not going to have very much impact on the quality or utility of evaluation research. Rather, we stress that this is the time when sponsors and conductors of evaluation research together must take drastic steps to improve the state of the art and the utilization of evaluation research. Some of our specific recommendations may not be the wisest ones possible, but we are convinced that a comprehensive strategy to improve endeavors in the field is required.

Third, we believe that while our review may not be the model for future studies of the work of social scientists and their relationships to sponsoring organizations, this is an area which demands future research and future research support. It is often said that lawyers rarely have wills and physicians often do not take annual physicals. At the present time, certainly, social science investigators are remiss in studying themselves.

This report, although highly technical in places, is frankly intended as a political document—a catalyst for social change. For at considerable cost, current evaluation research seems to be failing to live up to its promise.

Agencies Audited

Department of Health, Education and Welfare (HEW)
    Secretary's Office
    Office of Education (OE)
    National Institutes of Health (NIH)
    National Institute of Mental Health (NIMH)
    National Center for Health Services Research and Development
      (NCHSRD)
    Social Rehabilitation Service (SRS)
    Social Security Administration (SSA)
Department of Labor (DL)
    Manpower Programs
    Contract's Office
Department of Justice (D.J.)
    LEAA Program
Department of Housing and Urban Development (HUD)
    Model Cities Program
    Research and Demonstration Programs
Department of Agriculture (D.A.)
    Contract and Grants Program
Office of Economic Opportunity (OEO)
National Science Foundation

Survey on Evaluation Studies
of Social Action Programs

This survey is part of Russell Sage Foundation's program on the utilization of applied research. The purpose of this questionnaire is to obtain information on the scope and method of evaluation studies. The questionnaire is being sent to a systematically selected group of investigators whose grants or contracts received Federal support in fiscal year 1970, and which granting agencies have identified as evaluation studies. The selected studies focus on either the description or assessment of service, treatment, intervention, or social change programs. Evaluation studies are included in the fields of education, manpower, health, income security, public safety and housing.

> Information is requested in connection with the following grant or contract:

Both in government and the research community, the term evaluation is loosely defined and there is wide variation in what constitutes evaluation research. Throughout the questionnaire the term *evaluation study* is used to refer to the different types of research investigations that are directed at assessing either the implementation of social action programs or their impact. Evaluation studies are often categorized as field experiments, demonstration-research projects, and action-research programs. Also, for purposes of this study, the term *action program* is used throughout this questionnaire to refer to the wide range of service, treatment, intervention, and social change programs that are the focus of evaluation studies.

Information is requested only on the evaluation aspects of the study identified by the grant or contract noted above. If the Federal evaluation funds are not separable from other support, please provide the information in terms of the entire project.

The Foundation study has been developed in collaboration with a number of groups and persons in the Federal government. However, it is being undertaken independently, and supported solely by Russell Sage Foundation funds. The results will be made public through the Foundation's regular publication program, but individual responses will remain unidentified. All publications concerning the findings of the study will be distributed to cooperating Federal agencies and participants in the study.

ORGANIZATIONAL CHARACTERISTICS

The first section of this questionnaire is concerned with characteristics of the specific organization undertaking the evaluation study and the relationship between it and the particular organization undertaking the social action program.

1. Which of the following best describes the organizational arrangements under
(11) which the evaluation study is being conducted?

___1 Evaluation and action components conducted by the same organization

___2 Evaluation and action components partly or completely conducted by different organizations

___3 Evaluation and action components conducted by different organizations where one is a subcontractor of the other

___4 Evaluation and action components both subcontractors of a third organization

___5 Other (Specify)_____

2. If the same organization is conducting *BOTH* the action and evaluation
(12) programs, are they being undertaken by:

☐ Check here (and do not answer question) if evaluation and action being conducted by different organizations.

___1 The same persons

___2 Some are same persons and some different persons

___3 Different persons

3. Are there other organizations who are contractors or subcontractors for parts
(13) of the evaluation component of the contract or grant?

___1 Yes ___2 No

4. How would you best characterize the relationship between the social action
(14) group or groups, if independent of the evaluation team, and the evaluation team?

☐ Check here (and do not answer remainder of question) if evaluation and action conducted by the same persons or a single group.

___1. Relationship between evaluation team and action group(s) confined to fiscal and related administrative decisions with conduct of research primarily determined by evaluation team.

___2. Formal reporting and review of major research decisions by the action group(s), but actual conduct of research determined by the evaluation team.

___3. Joint planning and decision making for the conduct of the research by the by the action group(s) and the evaluation team.

___4. Close supervision of research activities and major decisions in conduct of research undertaken by the action group(s).

___5. Other (specify)_____

5. Who is the person currently (or at the time the project was completed) respon-
(15-sible for the administration and the direction of the evaluation study?
17)

Name _____   Address _____

Area Code   Phone Number   Current Organization

City   State   Zip

6. If the person named in question number 5 did not fill out this questionnaire, please specify respondent's

_____
(Name)   (Telephone Number)

7. Select the classification that best describes the organization undertaking the
(18) evaluation.
    ____1   Profit-making corporation
    ____2   Non-profit-making corporation or research institute
    ____3   University or other educational institution
    ____4   Private foundation
    ____5   Public agency or department
    ____6   Social service or social welfare planning agency
    ____7   Other (specify) _____

8. How many full-time (or full-time equivalents) persons are employed by the organ-
(19) ization checked in question #7?
    ____1   4 or less   ____5   50- 99
    ____2   5- 9   ____6   100-300
    ____3   10-19   ____7   over 300
    ____4   20-49

9. What is the status of the social action program and the evaluation study?

Evaluation Study (20)		Action Program (21)
____1	In progress	____1
____2	Completed	____2
____3	Terminated without completion	____3
____4	Other (specify)_____	____4

If your study is not an evaluation study, i.e., it is not a description or assessment of an action program, stop here and check ☐. Please return the questionnaire.

CHARACTERISTICS OF THE STUDY

10. With which one of the following areas is the evaluation study primarily concerned? If the study focuses on more than one area, indicate the primary area in the left-hand column and the others in the right-hand column.

Primary Concern (22-23)		Additional Concerns
	____CHECK HERE IF ONLY ONE CONCERN	
____01	Health (except Mental Health)	____(24)
____02	Mental Health	____(25)
____03	Education	____(26)
____04	Manpower Training	____(27)
____05	Income Security	____(28)
____06	Crime Control and Prevention	____(29)
____07	Delinquency	____(30)
____08	Housing	____(31)
____09	Aging	____(32)
____10	Physical Rehabilitation	____(33)
____11	Other (Specify) _____	____(34)

11. Which of the following categories describes best the population or scope of the study? If the population or scope of the action program is different from that of the evaluation study, indicate in the right-hand column. Check all that apply.

Evaluation Study		Action Program
		___CHECK HERE IF SAME AS EVALUATION STUDY
___(37)	National	___(48)
___(38)	Regional	___(49)
___(39)	Statewide	___(50)
___(40)	Metropolitan Area	___(51)
___(41)	Citywide	___(52)
___(42)	Urban Neighborhood	___(53)
___(43)	Suburban Community	___(54)
___(44)	Rural	___(55)
___(45)	Other_____	___(56)
___(46)		___(57)
___(47)		___(58)

12. Describe briefly the primary problem or condition that the action program is
(59-designed to improve, modify, or change:_____
60)
_____

13. Action programs may focus on one or more of the following units as the targets for change.
   a. The targets for change are persons or groups who are regarded as either deviant or problem individuals, such as delinquents or the handicapped, or persons affected by problem individuals, such as families of alcoholics, or persons who are the objects of undesirable activities or conditions, such as the victims of a crime, poverty, and racial discrimination.
   b. The targets for change are professionals or other individuals who provide services and treatment, or the organizations in which they work (e.g., modifying the treatment practices of psychiatrists or changing the operations of a hospital out-patient clinic).
   c. The targets for change are physical objects or territorial units such as housing conditions, recreational facilities, or neighbohoods.

Which of these types of units are the foci of the evaluation study? If the units for the action program are different, use the right-hand column as well. Check all that apply.

Evaluation Study	Units	Action Program
		___CHECK HERE IF SAME AS EVALUATION STUDY
___1 Yes ___2 No (61)	a. Deviant or problem person, groups, or victims	___1 Yes ___2 No (64)
___1 Yes ___2 No (62)	b. Providers of service	___1 Yes ___2 No (65)
___1 Yes ___2 No (63)	c. Physical objects, or territorial units	___1 Yes ___2 No (66)

14. Over the life of the evaluation study, what is the number of units involved in it, i.e. size of study group or sample? Since some programs have several study populations, such as children and parents, or heating units and electric appliances, space has been left for description of several groups (and the corresponding size of each study group).

Description of units (e.g., parents, dwellings)		Number	
a. _____	(67-68)	_____	(69)
b. _____	(70-71)	_____	(72)
c. _____	(73-74)	_____	(75)
d. _____	(76-77)	_____	(78)

> **If only physical objects or territorial units (i.e., you checked only c to question 13) are included in the study, check here and go to question number 24.** ☐

15. Check as many of the following descriptions of study units that apply to your project. If the units of the action program are different than those of the evaluation study, use the right-hand column.

Evaluation Study	Units	Action Program
		____CHECK HERE IF SAME AS EVALUATION STUDY
__1 Yes ____2 No (7)	Individuals are the unit	__1 Yes ____2 No (10)
__1 Yes ____2 No (8)	Small groups such as street gangs or families are the unit	__1 Yes ____2 No (11)
__1 Yes ____2 No (9)	Formal organizations, agencies or incorporated groups are the unit	__1 Yes ____2 No (12)

Questions 16 through 23 are designed to obtain information on the social characteristics of the units, persons, or groups included in your evaluation study. Since several target populations may be included, space has been provided with letters (a, b, c, and d) to correspond to groups you identified in question 14.

16. What are the ages of the persons studied? Check all that apply.

Age		Target Populations			
		a	b	c	d
Under 1 year	(13-16)	____1	____1	____1	____1
1 to 4 years	(17-20)	____2	____2	____2	____2
5 to 8 years	(21-24)	____3	____3	____3	____3
9 to 14 years	(25-28)	____4	____4	____4	____4
15 to 18 years	(29-32)	____5	____5	____5	____5
19 to 25 years	(33-36)	____6	____6	____6	____6
26 to 50 years	(37-40)	____7	____7	____7	____7
51 to 65 years	(41-44)	____8	____8	____8	____8
Over 65 years	(45-48)	____9	____9	____9	____9
All ages	(49-52)	____10	____10	____10	____10
No information		____11	____11	____11	____11

17. What is the educational status of the persons studied?

Educational Status	a (53)	b (54)	c (55)	d (56)
Some currently in school	____1	____1	____1	____1
Very few currently in school	____2	____2	____2	____2
No one currently in school	____3	____3	____3	____3
All currently in school	____4	____4	____4	____4
No information	____5	____5	____5	____5

18. What is the *average* amount of schooling of the persons studied?

Education	a (57)	b (58)	c (59)	d (60)
Less than 6th grade	____1	____1	____1	____1
6th to 11th grade	____2	____2	____2	____2
Completed high school	____3	____3	____3	____3
Some college	____4	____4	____4	____4
Completed college	____5	____5	____5	____5
Graduate or professional education	____6	____6	____6	____6
All education levels	____7	____7	____7	____7
No information	____8	____8	____8	____8

19. What is the work status of the group being studied?

Work Status	a (61)	b (62)	c (63)	d (64)
Most currently working full-time	___1	___1	___1	___1
Some currently working full-time	___2	___2	___2	___2
Very few currently working full-time	___3	___3	___3	___3
No one currently working full-time	___4	___4	___4	___4
No information	___5	___5	___5	___5

20. What is the *typical* occupation of the persons studied?

Occupation	a (65)	b (66)	c (67)	d (68)
Unskilled	___1	___1	___1	___1
Skilled and semi-skilled blue collar	___2	___2	___2	___2
Clerical and sales	___3	___3	___3	___3
Managerial	___4	___4	___4	___4
Professional	___5	___5	___5	___5
Welfare recipients	___6	___6	___6	___6
Study group too young to work	___7	___7	___7	___7
No single occupation predominates	___8	___8	___8	___8
No information	___9	___9	___9	___9

21. What is the *modal* income of the households of the persons studied?

Income	a (69)	b (70)	c (71)	d (72)
Over 15,000 dollars	___1	___1	___1	___1
10,000 to 14,999 dollars	___2	___2	___2	___2
5,000 to 9,999 dollars	___3	___3	___3	___3
2,000 to 4,999 dollars	___4	___4	___4	___4
Under 2,000 dollars	___5	___5	___5	___5
No income group predominates	___6	___6	___6	___6
No information	___7	___7	___7	___7

22. Does any single group predominate among the persons studied?

Group	a (73)	b (74)	c (75)	d (76)
Whites	___1	___1	___1	___1
Blacks	___2	___2	___2	___2
Orientals	___3	___3	___3	___3
Spanish-speaking persons	___4	___4	___4	___4
American Indians	___5	___5	___5	___5
No group predominates	___6	___6	___6	___6
No information	___7	___7	___7	___7

23. Is the study group primarily males, females, or about equally distributed?

Sex	a (7)	b (8)	c (9)	d (10)
Primarily males	___1	___1	___1	___1
Primarily females	___2	___2	___2	___2
About equally distributed	___3	___3	___3	___3
No information	___4	___4	___4	___4

SCOPE OF ACTION PROGRAM

24. Is there an overall perspective, theory, or frame
of reference that guides the action program
that you are studying? ___1 Yes ___2 No (11)

IF YES, describe:_____(12-13)

_____

_____

25. Briefly describe the elements, practices, or procedures of the action program that you are studying. Alongside of each, identify the specific objective or anticipated outcomes for which these procedures were implemented.

Example: Elements   Objectives

Teaching machine   *To improve reading*

Extra guidance counseling   *To increase motivation*

Elements   Objectives

a. _____ (14-15)   _____ (16-17)

b. _____ (18-19)   _____ (20-21)

c. _____ (22-23)   _____ (24-25)

d. _____ (26-27)   _____ (28-29)

e. _____ (30-31)   _____ (32-33)

f. _____ (34-35)   _____ (36-37)

EVALUATION PROCEDURES

This section is concerned with the procedures utilized to assess whether or not the action program is implemented according to program specifications and guidelines. Questions also are included on whether or not the evaluation study included measurement of impact or change.

ASSESSMENT OF PROGRAM IMPLEMENTATION

26. Does the evaluation study include any procedures to examine whether or not the action program is being carried out in accordance with program specifications and guidelines?

    ____1 Yes   ____2 No (38)

If no to question 26, skip to question 33

---

27. Which of the following procedures are used to examine whether or not the action program is being carried out in accordance with the program specifications and guidelines? Check all categories that apply.

    ____1 (39)   Participant or semi-participant observation

    ____1 (40)   Review of reports and records of action agency

    ____1 (41)   Reports and records of action agency collected especially for evaluation study

    ____1 (42)   Interviews or questionnaire with professionals or other providers of service

    ____1 (43)   Information from recipients of services

    ____1 (44)   Reports of persons in community with knowledge of program

    ____1 (45)   Other (specify)_____

28. How are the data recorded that are used to assess program specifications and guidelines? Check all categories that apply.

    ____1 (46)   On structured questionnaires or interviews

    ____1 (47)   In narrative form by category according to an outline or data guide

    ____1 (48)   In narrative form as case history or process recording

    ____1 (49)   Other (specify)_____

29. For purposes of assessing whether or not the action program is being carried out in accordance with program specifications and guidelines, are all of the units that are the target of the action program examined or observed, or are they sampled? (Units may be persons, groups, organizations, providers of service, or physical objects).

____1 (50)   All observed

____2   Sampled

IF SAMPLED, describe the sampling procedure briefly:(51-52)_____

_____

_____

30. Are those units that are examined or observed followed all of the time or sampled (53) at different points in time?

____1   Observed all the time

____2   Sampled at points in time

____3   Sampled only one time

IF SAMPLED AT POINTS IN TIME, briefly describe the procedure:(54)_____

_____

_____

31. Does the analysis of the data include any of the following techniques? Check all that apply.

____(55)   Multivariate statistical procedures

____(56)   Simple descriptive statistical procedures

____(57)   Ratings from qualitative data including case reports and
             observation material

____(58)   Narrative descriptive reports

____(59)   Impressionistic summaries

____(60)   Other (specify)_____

32. If asked to characterize your analysis of data as quantitative or qualitative, how (61) would you describe it?

____1   Quantitative

____2   Qualitative

____3   About evenly divided

MEASUREMENT OF IMPACT OR CHANGE

33. Does the evaluation study include procedures to measure the impact or changes (62) that may occur because of the action or intervention program?

____1 Yes   ____2 No

If no to question 33, skip to question 42

---

34. Does the research plan to measure impact or change include an experimental (63) or quasi-experimental design?

____1 Yes   ____2 No

If no to question 34, skip to question 37

---

35. Does the experimental design include control or comparison groups that are (64) either not exposed to any action program or who receive different interventions than the experimental program being evaluated?

____1 Yes   ____2 No

IF YES, do the evaluation researchers assign cases to experimental and control or comparison groups on a random or probability basis?(65)

____1 Yes   ____2 No

36. Does the experimental design include data collected at different points in time (66) or only at one point in time?

 ____1 After the action program
 ____2 During the action program
 ____3 Before and after the action program
 ____4 During and after the action program
 ____5 Before, during, and after the action program

37. Instead of or in addition to an experimental design, are any of the following approaches utilized? Check all that apply.

 ____1 (67) Longitudinal study without control or comparison groups
 ____1 (68) Cross-sectional study without control or comparison groups
 ____1 (69) Comparison of experimental study group with available secondary data
 ____1 (70) Description of processes or practices in relationship to expert judgments
 ____1 (71) Other (specify)_____

38. Which of the following procedures are used to collect data on impact or change? Check all that apply.

 ____1 (72) Participant or semi-participant observation
 ____1 (73) Review of service reports and records of action agency
 ____1 (74) Reports and records of action agency collected especially for evaluation study
 ____1 (75) Interviews or questionnaires with professionals and other providers of service in the action agency
 ____1 (76) Information from recipients of services
 ____1 (77) Reports of persons in community with knowledge of program
 ____1 (78) Other (specify)_____

39. How are the data to measure impact or change recorded? Check all that apply.

 ____1 (7) On structured questionnaires or interviews
 ____1 (8) In narrative form by category according to an outline or data guide
 ____1 (9) In narrative form as case history or process recording
 ____1 (10) Other (specify)_____

40. In order to assess impact or change, do the units studied (i.e., persons, groups, (11) organizations, providers of service, or physical objects) constitute the total population served by the action program, a sample of it, or is it composed of units different from those exposed to the action program?

 ____1 Total group served
 ____2 Sample of group served
 ____3 Different from group served
 ____4 Sample of group served and group not served
 If 2, 3, or 4 ABOVE, describe how selected: (12)

41. Describe briefly the criteria on which impact or change are studied. For example, improved housing conditions, increased reading skills, and so on. How are they measured?

Criteria		How Measured	
a. _____	(13-14)	_____	(15-16)
_____		_____	
b. _____	(17-18)	_____	(19-20)
_____		_____	
c. _____	(21-22)	_____	(23-24)
_____		_____	
d. _____	(25-26)	_____	(27-28)
_____		_____	
e. _____	(29-30)	_____	(31-32)
_____		_____	
f. _____	(33-34)	_____	(35-36)
_____			

EVALUATION STUDY PERSONNEL AND FUNDING

42. Regarding the evaluation study (*not* the action program), how many persons are
(37- included in your professional and technical staff (*not* including clerical workers)?
38) Add up part-time personnel and count as full-time equivalents, e.g., 5 full-time
plus 2 half-time = 6

_____

43. For each of the persons described below, check his appropriate field of specialization (if personnel changed, answer for current person or one at the end of the study):
   a. The person responsible for the conduct of the evaluation research. Most often this person is called the research director, the study director, or the project director.
   b. The person who is responsible for the administration and organization of the evaluation research unit in which the study is housed. This person typically is responsible for fiscal matters, personnel practices and other management functions. While he may have a number of titles, he is often referred to as the principal investigator, project administrator, division or unit director, or program director. He is the person to whom the project director reports.
   c. The single person (possibly a consultant) who on a *day-to-day basis* participates most fully in the evaluation effort and whose work is most *essential* to the evaluation study.

	a) Project Director (39-40)	b) Principal Investigator (41-42)	c) Person Most Essential to Evaluation Study on Daily Basis (43-44)
		____SAME AS PROJECT DIRECTOR	____SAME AS PROJECT DIRECTOR
			____SAME AS PRINCIPAL INVESTIGATOR
Anthropology	____01	____01	____01
Economics	____02	____02	____02
Education	____03	____03	____03

Engineering	____04	____04	____04
Law	____05	____05	____05
Medicine (except Psychiatry)	____06	____06	____06
Psychiatry	____07	____07	____07
Psychology	____08	____08	____08
Social Work	____09	____09	____09
Sociology	____10	____10	____10
Other_____	____11	____11	____11
specify			

44. For each of the persons described above, what is their highest earned degree and years of related research experience?

	a) Project Director	b) Principal Investigator	c) Person Most Essential to Evaluation Study on Daily Basis
Highest Degree	_____(45)	_____(46)	_____(47)
Years Experience	_____(48-49)	_____(50-51)	_____(52-53)

45. What are the dates of the initial grant for the evaluation program?

Starting Date   _____(54-55)
                                        (Month and Year)

Original Termination Date   _____(56-57)
                                        (Month and Year)

46. Has the grant been extended?(58)   ____1 Yes   ____2 No

IF YES, to what month and year?(59-60)   _____
                                         (Month)   (Year)

47. Was the action program in operation prior to the time the contract or grant was awarded for the evaluation research study?   ____1 Yes   ____2 No (61)
IF YES, how long?   _____Years before evaluation study (62)

48. Are there separate budget estimates for the action program and the evaluation (63) study?   ____1 Yes   ____2 No
IF YES AND KNOWN, indicate these amounts separately as well as the total amount:

	Evaluation Study (64-67)	Action Program (68-71)	Total (72-75)
Last complete fiscal year	$_____	$_____	$_____
Total project	$_____	$_____	$_____
	(7-10)	(11-14)	(15-18)

____Check Here if Separate Research and Action Budget Amounts Unknown

49. How would you best characterize the relationship between the agency funding (19) the evaluation study and the evaluation team?

____1. Relationship between evaluation team and funding agency confined to fiscal and related administrative decisions with conduct of research primarily determined by evaluation team.

____2. Formal reporting and review of major research decisions by the funding agency, but actual conduct of research determined by the evaluation team.

____3. Joint planning and decision making for the conduct of the research by the funding agency and the evaluation team.

____4. Close supervision of research activities and major decisions in conduct of research undertaken by the funding agency.

____5. Other (specify) _____

_____

_____

50. In addition to Federal funds, is the research supported by any other sources?
(20) ____1 Yes ____2 No

IF YES, what are the other sources? Check all that apply.

____1 (21) State Funds   ____1 (25) Profit making corporation
____1 (22) City Funds   ____1 (26) Non-paid personnel
____1 (23) Foundation   ____1 (27) Other (specify)_____
____1 (24) University Funds   ____1   No information

DISSEMINATION AND UTILIZATION OF FINDINGS OF EVALUATION STUDIES

The findings of evaluation efforts are communicated in a variety of ways and to different audiences. This final section focuses on both the plans for and the actual dissemination of the findings of your evaluation study.

51. What is the status of the evaluation?
(28) ____1 Data collection and analysis in progress
____2 Data collection and analysis completed, but not final write-up
____3 Completed, including final report
____4 Terminated without completion
____5 Other (specify) _____

52. Have any written reports of the findings of the evaluation study been completed? Check all that apply.
____1 (29) Yes, report with recommendations for the action program studied
____1 (30) Yes, report with recommendations for social policy in the area
of the study
____1 (31) Yes, report with recommendations for further research
____1 (32) Yes, preliminary or interim reports
____1 (33) Yes, informal working papers
____1 (34) No

53. In addition to any written reports that have been completed, what reports are planned? Check all that apply.
____1 (35) Report with recommendations for the action program studied
____1 (36) Report with recommendations for social policy in the area of
the study
____1 (37) Report with recommendations for further research
____1 (38) Preliminary or interim reports
____1 (39) Informal working papers
____1 (40) None

54. a. Does the evaluation grant or contract require the evaluation researcher to provide reports of the findings to any of the groups listed below?

Check Here if Reports Are Not Required ☐

b. Regardless of whether or not you are required to provide reports to one or more of the groups listed below, who is regarded by the evaluators as the major "consumer" for their findings?

c. In preparing evaluation reports, which group from those listed below are you most conscious of in terms of maximizing communication?

	a) Reports Required	b) Major Consumer	c) Maximizing Communication
Federal Elected Political Officials	____(41)	____(42)	____(43)
State and Local Political Officials	____(44)	____(45)	____(46)
Staff of Federal Agencies	____(47)	____(48)	____(49)
Staff of State and Local Government Agencies	____(50)	____(51)	____(52)
Action Program Personnel	____(53)	____(54)	____(55)
Other Evaluation Researchers	____(56)	____(57)	____(58)
University Affiliated Persons	____(59)	____(60)	____(61)
Community Groups	____(62)	____(63)	____(64)
General Public	____(65)	____(66)	____(67)
Mass Media	____(68)	____(69)	____(70)
Other (specify)	____(71)	____(72)	____(73)

55. What is the form of planned or completed reports? Check as many as apply.

☐ No Final Report Planned (7)

____1 (8)   Hard or softbound book or monograph
____1 (9)   Printed document by funding agency or organization conducting evaluation
____1 (10) Reproduced document over 25 copies
____1 (11) Reproduced document under 25 copies
____1 (12) Journal article
____1 (13) Mass media
____1 (14) Other (specify) _____

56. Aside from any written documents, have the findings of the evaluation study been communicated in any of the following ways? Check as many as apply.

____1 (15) Informal group discussion with funding agency personnel
____1 (16) Informal group discussion with action program personnel
____1 (17) Informal discussion with other evaluation researchers, or colleagues
____1 (18) Informal discussion with political or community groups or persons
____1 (19) Formal papers at professional meetings
____1 (20) Newspaper or magazine articles
____1 (21) Other (specify) _____

____1 (22) Not applicable

57. Check from among the list below any plans for the evaluation research group to communicate the findings? Check all that apply.

____1 (23) Informal group discussion with funding agency personnel
____1 (24) Informal group discussion with action program personnel
____1 (25) Informal discussion with other evaluation researchers or colleagues
____1 (26) Informal discussion with political or community groups or persons
____1 (27) Formal papers at professional meetings
____1 (28) Newspaper or magazine articles
____1 (29) Other (specify) _____

58. Have the findings of the evaluation study been communicated to community
(30) members most affected by the action program, including the persons involved as part of the target population?
____1 Yes   ____2 No
(31) IF NO, are there any plans to do so?   ____1 Yes   ____2 No

59. To whom are reports available? Check all that apply.
____1 (32) Any interested party
____1 (33) Persons of recognized professional standing
____1 (34) Persons in funding agency
____1 (35) Persons in action agency

60. Under what circumstances can reports of the evaluation study be released?
(36) ____1 Only with approval of funding agency
____2 Only with approval of action agency
____3 Only with approval of both
____4 No approval needed

61. Are there any time restrictions as to when the reports may be released?
(37)   ____1 Yes   ____2 No
(38) IF YES, please specify_____